A Heart Exposed

Talking to God with Nothing to Hide

Steven James

Revell
a division of Baker Publishing Group
Grand Rapids, Michigan

Published by Revell
a division of Baker Publishing Group
P.O. Box 6287, Grand Rapids, MI 49516–6287
www.revellbooks.com

Printed in the United States of America

Library of Congress Cataloging-in-Publication Data
James, Steven, 1969–
A heart exposed : talking to God with nothing to hide / Steven James.
p. cm.
Includes index.
ISBN 978-0-8007-3173-1 (pbk.)
1. Prayers. I. Title.
BV245.J36 2009
242.8—dc22 2009014439

The prayer on page 60 is based on a prayer in *Never the Same* by Steven James (Youth Specialties, 2005), page 41.

The prayer on page 87 is based on a prayer in *Praying from the Gut* (Standard Publishing), page 115.

The prayer on page 98 is based on a prayer in *Never the Same* by Steven James (Youth Specialties, 2005), pages 142–43.

In keeping with biblical principles of creation stewardship, Baker Publishing Group advocates the responsible use of our natural resources. As a member of the Green Press Initiative, our company uses recycled paper when possible. The text paper of this book is comprised of 30% post-consumer waste.

green press INITIATIVE

For Jacob, Caleb, and Dhanraj,
three men who serve the king

Thanks to

Liesl Huhn, Trinity Huhn, Pam Johnson, Dr. Mike Sweeney, Mark Collins, Bill Jolley, David Lehman, Pamela Harty, Kristin Kornoelje, and Jennifer Leep.

Introduction

I think prayer is the most profound, daring, authentic, mysterious communication available to the human heart, but even though I know how important prayer is, I don't feel particularly qualified to teach people how to do it.

Almost always my prayers tend to do one of three things: (1) tell God he's great, (2) ask him for stuff, (3) tell him I'm sorry.

One day I realized that when I talk to my friends, I do a lot more than compliment them, ask for things, and apologize. In fact, if that's all I did, it would be a pretty shallow friendship.

Instead, we talk about what's on our minds, our dreams and problems, our hobbies and struggles. We argue, we fight, we celebrate. Sometimes we laugh or complain or remember good times together. And sometimes we don't talk at all, we just hang out.

God offers me this kind of deep friendship, but I rarely take him up on his offer.

In contrast to my limited prayer vocabulary, the prayers of the people in Scripture contain everything from desperate cries for mercy to powerful stories of deliverance to outbursts of praise to incisive observations about the injustices of life.

The Psalms are full of complaints, moments of amazement, and whispered pleas that throb with grief and pain and raw, human need. In this ancient collection of prayers, we find imagery, theology, intimacy, fear, worry, love, and wonder, and also broken hearts, broken dreams, and broken lives—and healed ones too.

Joy.

Awe.

Glory.

Terror.

And almost always, the prayers go deeper than "You're awesome, God," "Please help me, God," or "I'm sorry, God."

The prayers in the Bible strike me as being deep and real, lofty and glorious, painful and frolicking—just like I want my prayers to be.

And just like I want my friendship with God to be too.

As I've worked on this book, I've found that often my most genuine, heartfelt prayers are a little messy, a little rough around the edges, and sometimes a little awkward, because that's what my life is like and that's what God asks me to bring him.

Polished, eloquent, impressive prayers have a tendency to become performances. Real prayer is more concerned with honesty, pain, and amazement than getting all the words just right.

So as we pray, I think we need to be willing to reveal our vulnerabilities and our passions, our sorrow and our joy, our shameful secrets and pet temptations, and our most intimate desires and dreams.

I'm hoping this book will help you do that.

I should mention that I believe written prayers have just as vital a place in our lives as extemporaneous, or spontaneous, prayers do. After all, if our ancestors hadn't written down their prayers we wouldn't have the greatest collection of prayers in the world—the book of Psalms.

Also, most of our contemporary worship and praise songs are prayers that have been set to music. Each one is carefully written and crafted by songwriters and musicians to lead us into closer communion with God. While it's true that some churches improvise their worship lyrics, I think it's safe to say that most do not. So here's my question to those who shy away from written prayers: why shouldn't the prayers we speak be as carefully prepared as the ones we sing?

It might be helpful to know why I didn't include section headings (such as Prayers of Thanks, Prayers of Confession, Prayers of Praise, etc.) or titles for the prayers. I left them out for four reasons:

1. Nearly all other prayer books I've looked at do that, so it seemed too formulaic to me.
2. When I experimented with including them and gave copies of the book to some friends to read, they told me that titling the prayers was distracting and sometimes confusing. After looking over the prayers, I agreed with them.
3. I never label the prayers I spontaneously offer to God, and it felt contrived to do so on the page.
4. Many of the prayers could have easily fit into more than one category, and placing them in one section rather than another limited their meaning. Categorizing them boxed them in, so to speak. But one of my reasons for writing this book was to help myself, and you, step out of our typical cookie-cutter conversations with God, instead of remaining locked in them.

I'm sure there'll be some prayers in this book that you just don't connect with, but I'm hoping that most of the time you'll find the prayers expressing something real in your life.

As I write this, I'm saying a prayer of my own: first, that the words on these pages would not simply form a book but would open a space for you to encounter more of God's presence.

And second, that the words wouldn't get in the way of the silences between them—that as you pray, you'll be able to hear the God of the universe whispering peace to you as you offer him your bare-naked heart.

Steven James

this moment is all that you ask of me.
i can either give it to you,
or turn it into a fist and
try to keep it to myself.

and fail.

Jesus, your prayers were drenched
with sweat and blood,
    and throbbed with glory and pain.
My prayers are so often soaked in perfume,
decorated with nothing more
than stock phrases and catchy clichés—
carefully varnished pieces of furniture
    for you to admire.

Unpeel my pretenses, masks, and façades,
and stare beneath my whitewashed life.
Shake off the rust,
and the dust,
and the tired repetition.

Here, now, Jesus,
I will break the trend,
I will speak prayers raw with the realities of life,
tender with the realization of grace;
prayers
with flesh and blood,
    born of both marvel and pain.

Prayers like yours.

God's word is living and active. It is sharper than any two-edged sword
and cuts as deep as the place where soul and spirit meet, the place where joints and marrow meet.
God's word judges a person's thoughts and intentions.

—Hebrews 4:12

O Ruthlessly Gracious One,
I'm slowly learning that
mercy is the most painful gift to receive.

Why does your grace have to glisten
on the edge
of an arrowhead?

It'd be so much more convenient if the cure came
in a pill or a bottle or a nice little self-affirmation
that I could repeat to myself every day.

So now,
you raise the bow and wink at me
as if you're enjoying this.

I see the bowstring tremble and then,
as the string slips through your fingers,
I watch the arrow fly with swift precision
and feel it hit me, square in the gut.

It cuts
through the womb of who I am
so that I can be reborn.
at last.

Lord of the broken oak branch,
Lord of the avenues,
Tweak and restartle me, guide my hand.
—from *Negative Blue* by Charles Wright

To the Nazarene.

I dance through life.
I have my favorite partners:
now delight, now regret, now relief,
now despair.

But this time, as the music stirs,
I see your hand outstretched,
inviting me into the new song,
the glory song.

How long will you be willing to stand
on the dance floor
waiting for my answer?

i have seen it in others
and glimpsed it in myself—
when i disappear, i finally
begin to glow.

Savior,
as night fades,
as morning comes,
I take some time to prepare for today.
I know at times I'll be tempted to lose my patience.
At times I'll be tired,
at times people will push me to the edge,
at times I'll forget about you.

Frame my day around obedience,
cover my moments with a little more peace,
guide my words toward a little more graciousness,
and keep my thoughts revolving
a little more around you.

This day is a gift, and it may be my last.
So, with that thought in mind,
I step into this moment
holding your hand
and entering my day.

i have a
divine appointment
with the carpenter today.
i wonder what he's planning
to build,
    and whose turn it
will be to hold the hammer.

O Creator of Beating Hearts,
and Healer of Broken Ones,
I've let my passion grow cold
since those days
when I first began my journey
with you.

You've become a part of my life
rather than the center of it,
a distraction rather than the direction.
    And my prayers have grown stale,
stored so conveniently
in the cupboard of my heart.

So here's what I ask:
    give me the eyes of a newborn believer;
introduce yourself to me again.
Amaze me with your presence
and upset the comfortable balance
of my numb and stable life
with your strange brand
of fiery grace.

Crack open my courage and my awareness
so that I can finally speak to you
with all of my will and emotions,
with heartfelt needs and honest fumbling,
instead of holding myself back and
offering up such
    hollow little prayers.

Jesus,
you ate darkness for dessert.
and now i see you
offering me the fork.

Master of the Impossible,
I've noticed that only adults
carry their emptiness around with them.
Children seem to have found a way,
(or maybe simply remember how)
to set the shallowness down.

Today I want to be a child.

So here are my worries, God,
here are my cares.
I place them at your feet.

And now, a moment.
A gift.
A possibility.

"Take my yoke upon you," you told me.
And so I do.
And when I do,
I find a different kind of heaviness—
one that lifts me higher
than I could have ever climbed on my own.

living, breathing deity,
immigrant from heaven,
you spin the future on your finger,
but when you cry, you show
just how human
you really are.

To the only one who sees the world as it is.

I ask for clarity;
and if not clarity, purity,
and if not purity, forgiveness—
  not because I am so blind,
but because I'm so unwilling to open my eyes.

Where I've strayed, draw me in,
where I've stumbled, lift me up,
and where I've lifted myself,
  knock me down
until I see your world
and your love
with clear, unclouded eyes.

"He stretches out his heavens over empty space.
He hangs the earth on nothing whatsoever.
He holds the water in his thick clouds,
and the clouds don't even split under its weight. . . .
These are only glimpses of what he does.
We only hear a whisper of him!
Who can understand the thunder of his power?

—Job, arguing with his friends
about God's power (Job 26:7–14)

Earth-walking God,
you are elegant in your simplicity,
unequaled in your majesty,
exultant in your mystery.

"Consider the lilies," you said.
And when I actually
take the time to do it,
I notice the touch of your
beauty, the daintiness of a new day,
and promises as sweet as spring.

"Consider the ravens," you said.
So I do.
I consider them.
Their freedom, their grace,
the intricacy of their airy dance.
I see your hand upon them
and beyond them.

All around me, the world is speaking parables
but I rarely take the time
to listen.

So here I am,
leaning close to the day and listening to the world,
wake me up to hear nature whisper
the unspeakable name—
    your name.
And open my eyes to see
your terrible beauty reflected in the stars.

time has become my shackle
rather than my walking stick.
free me so that we might walk together
toward dawn.

To the one who is the way.

Though I'm on my way to heaven,
I'm still traveling through the land of lostness.
You called it the valley of the shadow of death,
which means it is also the pathway
    to the light of life.

The tendrils of darkness tug at my feet,
but I turn my eyes to the
    promised land.

And take another step through the valley of today.

whatever moon and rain may be
the hearts of men are merciless.
—James Wright, poet

Jesus,
it's a strange kind of reliance,
  this trust-thing is.
A way of finding security
by loosening my grip,
and discovering new strength
by leaning on you.

Here is the truth that I am so
hesitant to admit:
  all that's being born anew in me
comes from you.

This reawakening is my Calvary,
and my joy.

hell is the wound that never heals.
heaven is the party that never comes
to an end.

O God of outcasts, liars and thieves,
in a distant land, long ago,
you turned once upon a time
into happily ever after,
but only after you
left the palace,
became a peasant,
battled the dragon,
found the tower,
slashed through the hedge,
arrived at the side
    of the sleeping princess,
and
with
a kiss
toppled the curse
and awakened her at last,
and took her hand,
and invited everyone in the land—
    the rich and the poor,
    the paupers and the princes,
    the knights and the peasants and the whores,
    and me
to the wedding.

The curse is over,
the forever-story has
finally begun.

You say, "I'm rich. I'm wealthy. I don't need anything."
Yet, you do not realize that you are miserable,
pitiful, poor, blind, and naked.

—Jesus talking to the believers
in Laodicea (Revelation 3:17)

Clother of Naked Souls,

Adam and Eve fled naked through the garden,
found secret crannies in the shadows
and, with fingers still stained with the forbidden,
    wove together clothes to try and hide from you,
the one who sees all.

I see myself there, with them,
hiding from you,
trying to sew together some new way of life,

trying to escape the memory of the fruit
that tasted so good.
    Only a moment ago.

Seek me in my hiddenness
find me once again.

Your grace will clothe
even the deepest kinds
of fruit-inflicted shame.

---

if God cannot be found in laughter
he cannot be found at all.

O Wind of Truth,
O Breath of Comfort,
O Spirit of the Living God,
you have sought me through
time and space;
captured, enraptured me with your love.
Now the earth chains lay heavy
    around my feet.
What else can I do?
I blossom at your touch.

the vultures of doubt
pluck away at my faith-flesh
and i am too weak
to swat them away.

Mighty Deliverer,
you conquered by dying,
you led by serving,
you lifted others,
    by lowering yourself.
You are a paradox
I will never understand.

You ask me to hold on,
and to let go;
to shed the past,
and to put on the future;
to fix my eyes on the unseen rather than the seen,
to know a love that surpasses knowledge,
and to lean on what I cannot prove
    in order to receive what I cannot earn.

You invite me to stop trying so hard
    and be perfect instead;
and when I fail, to stop feeling guilty
    and simply be forgiven.

I want to understand you,
    but I can't.
And when I try to wrap my mind around you,
    I fail.
You are the mystery I will never grasp,
offering a puzzling comfort
I cannot live without.

Cast celebration like a seed.
—from "The Big House,"
a poem by
Jonathan Williams

To the holy one.

What is worship?
What does it mean for me to bring you
the offering of my life?

Passion.
Illumination.
Fire that consumes, cleanses,
renews.

Fire that frees and ignites,
spark and blaze and licking flame.
This is the journey
from dust to fire,
desert to spring,
from cold coal
to flaming glory.

Worship begins with a single note
and ends with an all new melody.

Draw me deeper into the song.

"deliver us from evil"
more often than not
means "deliver us
from me."

To the source of joy.

Every man who sleeps in the arms
of a prostitute tells himself
that he is special in her eyes,
when all he is to her
is a paycheck.

I'm also an expert at using other people
until we're both used up.

I confess my self-centeredness to you.

Have mercy on me.

save me from the comfort
of my pillowed excuses
which keep trying to smother me
when i'm not looking.

Disturber of Sleep,
night crawls into me,
and whispers my name.
I can feel it worming through my heart.

But I see dawn breaking again
scratching at the moment,
inviting me to stop this game of
me-ness
and turn my eyes outward
to look at the world,
at the life,
at the glory,
that's bigger than me,
and is waiting so patiently
for the day when I'll finally be healed
of my carefully cultivated
    blindness.

the pen you use to write your
name upon my soul
looks suspiciously like
a sword.

To the one who brings sight to the blind
and good news to the poor.

Today I've got a sour taste
in my heart.
I've tried washing it out with all the usual products—
rationalizations and distractions and denial,
self-destruction and blame—
all these familiar ways
of condoning myself.
And even though I'm usually pretty good at it,
today something isn't right.
Or maybe something finally is.

As my excuses drop away,
I find myself with a renewed thirst for you.

the shape of each leaf is a mystery
too deep to comprehend.
a million miracles surround me
while i complain that there's
not enough room for cream in my espresso.

To the one who brings meaning to everything.

Why am I so obsessed with the trivial?
I'm addicted to the mirage
and blind to the true well
of living water
    bubbling at my feet.

Help me to be where I am,
present in the moment,
    in this moment,
doing only your will,
desiring nothing other than your glory.

They said, "Let's build a city for ourselves and a tower with its top in
the sky. Let's make a name for ourselves so that we won't become scattered all over the face of the earth."

—Moses writing about the people who built the Tower of Babel (Genesis 11:3–4)

To the artist of the universe.

Brick upon brick
the dark tower rose
like a fist thrust up against
heaven, defying
your high glory.

Then you shook your
head and said,
"Look what they're up to
now. Another tower in
honor of themselves.
Another 'impressive
accomplishment' that they
'can be proud of.'
So typical of my children,
always trying to be remembered,
always trying to leave a legacy behind.
Always getting things backward."

So you let their language become
as confused as their priorities
and all the tiny people
began to fumble around
and babble to each other
in words that sound
surprisingly
like mine.

how can i avoid despair
when i dare to peek at the truth
without the veil of
grace?

To the invisible one.

People say you're beautiful,
and I imagine your beauty is unsurpassed,
    stunning and glorious and sweet.

But still,
I've never seen your face,
only glimpsed your reflection
in clouds and stars and
infants' eyes.

With beauty beyond my grasp,
let me be content
experiencing your presence
rather than seeing your face.

Let that be enough,
    for now,
until I have heaven-born eyes.

if we have found peace,
it is only because
we have found
the end of
self.

To the giver, from the receiver.

I know so very little about love.
I like to think of it as pure and noble and kind,
but all too often it's messy
and sticky and has bruised knees
and scraped knuckles.

I see a young mother learning about love,
about the getting-up-in-the-middle-of-the-night
kind of love,
the diaper-changing love,
the dream-deferring love,
and I see that she finds a certain joy
in this love
    and a certain irritation, too.

As I walk through the love lessons that
you send, I find joy and irritability as well.

But the process, that's what I need,
    even if I may not want it.
I need the painful journey of learning to love,
because without it
I'll remain safely encased
in sterile indifference.
    Only through your awkward lessons
of loving dirty people,
can I finally become myself.

whenever i try to find myself,
i end up heading in the wrong direction.

A parable.

"If you are quiet, truly quiet—not just with your mouth, but in your mind—you will hear God," said the spiritual teacher.

And so the students stilled their voices and quieted their souls and let themselves drift toward the place of desirelessness.

All day they meditated, seated on the cold, tiled floor.

And the next day.

And the next.

And finally on the evening of the fourth day, one student called out and leaped to his feet.

"What's wrong?" cried the other students, opening their eyes and leaving their meditations. "What happened?"

His face was pale. His breath, quick. "I was quiet. I was quiet in the deepest part of my mind and the stillest part of my soul. And I heard a voice speaking to me."

"Was it the voice of God!?" they asked excitedly.

"It was not God."

"Whose voice was it?"

The student who had been so quiet peered at the ground. "My own. At the core of who I am I sing songs only in praise of myself."

The rest of the students stared in disbelief.

"I was hoping for God, but all I found was more of myself," he said.

"Ah," said the teacher. "Then you were the quietest of all."

"In that case, I'll never be that quiet again," said the student. And he left the room and never came back.

from this side of the
looking glass
death seems like the final night.
"yes," i hear you say.
"but only from that side."

O Revealer of Hearts,
quiet the part of me
that's addicted to activity,
fill the part of me
that's been hollowed out
by my smoke-screen holiness,
and awaken the part of me that's so
deeply, deeply asleep.

When you gave the
invitation to be "born again"
you wanted the phrase to be a
lightning bolt,
and not a revivalist's cliché.

"Are you born again?"
"Of course."

"Are you being born anew?"
"Huh?"

We are so deeply asleep,
so deeply dead that if we're ever
going to wake up,
ever going to be born again,
we need you to prod us where it hurts.

The rebirthing happens in those rare moments
when I begin to shift
my eyes from myself to you,
my confidence from my own efforts
    to your grace,
and my attention from my accomplishments
to your cross.

It is only then that the rebirthing happens.

I'm hesitant to take the next step.
I need you.
Guide me toward my new birth
and end this stillborn life.

If he died for his enemies, just think what he will do for his friends.

—from *Commentary on Paul's Epistles*
by Ambrosiaster

Liberator,
the more you loosen the ropes
that have tied me down,
the higher I feel you lift me
    in your wings.

Please be gentle with me,
for I'm only now learning to fly,
and the ground has been my refuge
for so long.

here's the irony: my obsession
with being my own person is what divorces me
from becoming my true, authentic self.

O King,
Let me weep and dance before your throne
as undignified and unashamed as David,
with a naked heart,
a wild tongue,
scarred emotions,
and earthy desires.

Break the chains of my respectable tidy language,
set loose my awe and my squirrelly playfulness.

I need the freedom and humility
to cry in your arms,
and the courage
to shout your praise.

i'm in the middle
of the labyrinth again.
if i could find my way back to the
beginning by myself,
i wouldn't need you.

To the one who called himself The Way.

Sorrow burrows through me
  when I watch the news on CNN,
  when I listen to the measured voices
  of NPR reporters telling me about suicide
  bombers
with names I can't pronounce
in countries I've never heard of.

And, oh yes, another 60 people are dead,
an earthquake killed 10,000.
And a tsunami killed 200,000 more.

Sorrow burrows through me,
but only for an instant,
as I check my email and see the prayer requests
and then delete them because
I am really very busy getting things done—
  Important Things I Need To Do
  Right Now.

Sorrow burrows through me
when I finally see the world
that you see.

And because I've been so blind, I wonder if
sorrow burrows through
  you
when you look at me.

when i find myself in you
i find a new self
in me.

Lord,
today I choose your path.

Today I choose to spread light and not shadows,
grace and not pain,
love and not apathy,
peace and not anger,
deep delight and not sharp sorrow.

I choose to stand on the rock and not the sand,
to glory in you and not myself,
to lift others up and not push them down,
to leave boasting to those with
    more reasons to do it than I.

I choose to revel in thanksgiving rather than
    discontent,
to foster a sense of enoughness rather than moreness,
to pursue relationships rather than reputation,
to be attuned to needs and not just desires.

Here, I offer my heart and my longings,
my dreams and my priorities,
my goals and my habits,
my choices and opinions.

So in the strength that you offer,
and by the grace that you give,
    I offer my "yes" to you.
Hear it clearly.
Nothing and no one above you.
That is my pledge for today.

Turn to me and have mercy on me,
for I am alone and in deep distress.

—A prayer
of King David (Psalm 25:16,
New Living Translation)

Adopter of Orphaned Souls,
I want to close my shades
shut out the day
retire into myself
    and hide in the secret corner of my shame.
Where else can I go?

Dawn retreats out of reach
and topples off the edge of the world,
then grief opens its mouth and I step inside
and slide willingly down its throat.

Where are you when I need you so much?
Where have you gone?

I cry out to you, hoping you'll
find me and take me home,
hoping I won't have to wait
forever to see you smile again.

galaxy dust and sunlight
wept at your death
and bled from your skin,

while i bled from your heart.

Faith spoke to me.

"You want to give me feet so I can walk next to you along the path, so that you can touch my scarred hands and feel my side and know that I'm your companion. But alas! Then you'd have to clip my wings and I could no longer fly before you and show you the way. Then I could never soar so close to Truth. You want to limit me to what you can see and touch, taste and feel. But alas! Then you would turn me into nothing more than Knowledge, my distant and arrogant cousin."

"But I prefer knowing to believing," I said to Faith.

"Yes," she said. "You prefer walking hand in hand with Knowledge whom you can touch and caress and kiss and worship. You prefer the candle to the flame. The wood to the fire. The moon to the sun. For the wax and the wood and the moon are cold and still. And dead. They can be studied and measured and known . . . But the flame! The fire! The sun! You can't touch them or hold them. You can only see them from afar and say, 'Ah! That heat that I feel is enough for me. I'm drawn to the flame, but I must also keep my distance.'"

And a sting in my soul told me Faith's words were true.

"Do you see?" she said. "I'm the light that reflects off the moon and the flame that flickers in your candle. I'm the heat that's not content to be seen, only felt. And so I'm closer to your heart, but farther from your head. I'm closer to your soul, but farther from your body. As soon as I can be known, I can no longer be believed. As soon as I can be proven, I can no longer be trusted."

"But if I can't prove you, how can I know you?"

"I am the mystery that calls to you from the mountain. The voice that whispers to you in the night. Just beyond what you can know. Just beyond what you can prove—*Did you hear that?*—And you don't know, not for sure, but you think that perhaps you did. It is then, it is there, that I am born. In the gentle moment when imagination and hope hold hands. And that's where I dwell. Between proof and doubt. In the unmapped realm."

I felt the stirring to move beyond the map's boundaries, into the place beyond places. "Lead on, O Faith," I cried. "For now I realize that you are my soul's first love. Not Knowledge after all!"

And Faith took my hand and led me here.

To this day.

---

i tend to want to make my relationship with you a
democracy
when in reality it's a dictatorship
in which you allow me to act as i please.

Lord,
I regret many things,
but I do not regret this moment with you.
For it will have been a lifetime well-spent
to have lived this single moment
aware of your presence.

after the affair,
after the forgiveness,
it doesn't take me long
to start flirting again.

Conquerer of Death,
Now I am Eve,
biting the fruit.
Now I am Cain,
murdering my brother.
Now I am Rahab,
prostituting my body.

I left my nets to follow you,
I walked on the water to meet you,
I laid palm branches in front of your path,
knelt to kiss your soiled feet.

I am Pilate washing my hands of you,
Judas washing my soul of you,
a priest shouting to crucify you,
a soldier coming to kill you,
Barabbas watching you take my place.

I see you suffer.
I see you die.
I cradle your warm corpse in my arms.
I watch them place your body in the tomb.

And now the moment rips in half,
and I'm running to town to tell the others,
reaching with trembling fingers to touch your scars.
bowing to worship at the foot of your throne.

You are my brother.
You are my rescuer,
the one who loved the broken me.

anytime i make light of another person's pain
i show that the part of my life
that matters most
is not yet converted.

Spirit of Comfort,
you whisper hope to me in traffic jams
and in graveyards, and in frozen food aisles and
in my cubicle at work.
You travel through sunlight and sorrow
to wink at me.

If you really are in control of everything;
if you really do desire the best for all your children,
then how could what happens to me this moment
be anything other than a blessing,
however masterfully
  disguised?

I see you, a playful dancing God,
Hide and seek-ing me.

My answer is yes,
I'd like to come out and play.

life is so short
dawn is so near.

remind me.

i tend to forget it
on my way to the shower
every morning.

God,
let the world enthrall me,
    because tedium is the language of hell;
wonder, the harmony of heaven.

Jesus, you were never frantic.
You never rushed.
You never double-parked your camel and then
pushed your way to the
front of the line at the market
    to get your Christmas shopping done
    before five o'clock.

Sometimes I catch myself
just going through the motions
and not receiving all that each
moment has to offer,
and I just find ways
to keep myself busy all day
instead of passionately
pursuing you.

I'm broken,
I'm angry,
I'm amazed,
I'm lonely,
I'm in awe.

At times I'm struck
    by what I know can only be your grace.
At times I'm shocked
    by what appears to be your indifference.

With every step I am continually
beginning my journey.

you offer me the mystery
of a life slit open,
so that my veins can finally pump
kingdom blood.

Magnificent One,
here are the gifts you offer:
fierce kindness
and reckless love;
shattering truth
and a healing touch;
    rich, lovely comfort
for travel-weary souls,
and laughing acceptance
for outcasts and fools.

You have your own brand of love.
It's a far-reaching, far-ranging love
that invites me to climb over the fence
and step into the wide-open fields
of your grace.

Yield yourself up to Him; learn to see yourself as you are: vain and ambitious of the admiration of others; seeking to become their idol to gratify your own idolatry of self; jealous and suspicious beyond measure, and fast sinking into an abyss. You must make yourself familiar with these dreadful thoughts; it is only in this way that you can dissolve the charm that enslaves you.

—from *Avoid Self-Love* by Francois de Fenelon (1651–1715), priest and Christian mystic

To the one who will never be understood, but yet
understands.

I have heard preachers talk
about how important it is for us
to ask you into our hearts,
but I've never heard any of them talk
about asking you into our wills.

At the moment of faith you enter my heart,
at the moment of surrender you enter my will.
I remember the moment of the first miracle,
let this be the moment of the second.

achievements are the shiny rungs
of a ladder tilted toward myself.

To the God who saves.

When harsh is the path and rough is the way,
when I travel alone through the rush of the day,
then lend me your comfort, and help me to say,
"Lead on, O Lord, lead on."

When worries rise on every side,
and my day is shadowed by subtle pride,
and my heart is searching for a place to hide,
Lead on, O Lord, lead on.

Lead on through the darkness,
lead on through the night,
lead me back into wonder,
and back to delight.
Take my hand as I travel,
through the desert 'til dawn—
lead on, dear Savior,
lead on!

i have a red carpet in my heart,
that i could roll out for you,
but i usually reserve it for my own
personal use.

O Ancient One,
long ago
your people would
repent in sackcloth and ashes,
   rip their clothes, and pull out their hair.

I tend to repent in less dramatic ways:
   "Hey, God. I'm sorry about that.
   Thanks for forgiving me.
   Amen."
Quick and painless little confessions
so I can get back to watching reruns of Friends.

I can't even remember the last time
   I cried over my sin—
I mean, my actual sin,
not just the consequences of getting caught.
It's been so long since I've been sorry enough,
ashamed enough,
to lower my eyes and weep.

Let my past trouble me,
let my sin overwhelm me,
let me see how deeply,
how terribly I have fallen
and how far you journeyed
through the shadows
to find me.

Help me shed tears again.
Grace is meaningless without the stark
realization of how deeply rebellious
  my heart has been.

as famished as i am,
as hard as i search,
i rarely find
the right kind of food.

Shepherd,
the wolf whispered to me
and I listened.
He led me toward the cliffs
where I've seen so many
other sheep follow him before.

You left the ninety-nine and came searching for me,
  even though I left the pasture willingly.

I hear your voice and I look at the wolf's
comforting grin.

And I'm torn about what to do.

my deepest need is to desire you more,
and to need you even more
than i desire you.

Healer and Provider,
thanksgiving doesn't come naturally to me,
or maybe I should say,
taking the time out of My Busy
and Important Life
to tell someone I'm thankful
doesn't come naturally to me.

I tend to keep my thanks inside
where it evaporates with time.

So, here I am, bringing you
the thanks you deserve for offering me
a richer life now,
    a forever life to come,
a strength beyond myself,
a more creative spirit,
deeper, more life-affirming priorities,
expansive freedom,
vivid hope,
a different kind of peace,
and the taste of glory's flavor
on my tongue.

i knew you were zeus,
but until we met,
i didn't know you were
also cupid.

A prayer of thanks to you.

For breath and life,
for pleasure and heartaches,
for laughter and tears and smiles,
thank you.

For coming to earth,
for teaching the truth,
for living and leading,
for dying and rising,
thank you.

O Glorious One,
thank you.

For friends who care,
and sunsets to quiet my spirit,
and second chances at life,
here is my thanks,
here is my heart.

Words fail me,
but you can see the thanksgiving,
rising in my heart.

Thank you, Lord Jesus,
for loving and blessing
and rescuing me.

I love you.

Whoever calls on the name of the LORD *will be saved.*
—Joel 2:32

Father,
I've been trespassing again,
slowly making my way through
the Ten Commandments:
a little lust,
a little hatred,
a little gossip,
a little cussing now and then.

Some disrespect here and there,
a few white lies.

I'm an expert at trespassing
without ever going anywhere—
envy, when I read about
   what my former classmates are doing these days;
greed, when I realize
   how much really cool stuff I don't have;
pride, when I see
   what I've accomplished over the years
   through my own hard work and perseverance.

Trespasses.

I feel regret crawl to the surface.
I wish, oh how I wish,
  I had it all to do over again.

Deliver me from evil
and lead me into forgiveness.
Let your grace cover me
and let hope fill my wayward heart again.

in the stream that never rests
you are the rock that never changes.

To my true and constant friend.

I'm tempted to think about the good ol' days
when I dreamed of a bright new future,
where things weren't as hard and stressful
and frustrating as they are now.

Yet, with your presence being poured through time,
this day is as bright as any ever promised;
this moment is as rich as any ever given.

You pass me another handful of moments
and I watch them fall like petals around my feet.
  Let me catch them and take in the fragrance
that permeates every moment you send.

"He learned how to walk, stumbled and fell, cried for His milk, sweated blood in the night, was lashed with a whip and showered with spit, was fixed to a cross and died whispering forgiveness on us all."

—from *The Ragamuffin Gospel*
by Brennan Manning

A prayer to the stable-born king.

"Do this in remembrance of me."

A slaughtered lamb on an ancient altar,
on a splintered cross,
with a crown of thorns.
A slain Savior in the darkened day,
on a lonely hill,
between two thieves.
A bloody gift to give the damned,
to remind that life
is a sip away.

The mystery of a prince's death,
turned to glorious life,
and a sacrifice,
and a meal of grace.

Bloody wine.
Fleshy bread.
Broken.
Poured.

I remember.
Yes, I remember.

You.

very few people
are brave enough to be born;
very few people are
insane enough to be truly alive.
    so,
    please,
make me bravely insane.

Holy Spirit,
Sometimes I question your motives,
sometimes I have doubts about heaven.

It's not something I like to admit to anyone—
after all, most of my friends at church seem so sure
    of themselves:
    "You can know that you know that you know
    that you know that you're going to heaven."

And I wonder what it would be like
to have that kind of solidness;
    to lean so confidently on knowledge rather than
holding onto the feathery lightness of faith.

You ask us to lean on the unseen,
to live with one foot
in the supernatural
world all around us,
    and within us.

Faith,
not knowledge,
is evidence of the unseen.

Remind me that in your kingdom
the tables are turned,
certainty is a cloud,
and faith is the only solid place to stand.

The LORD is close to the brokenhearted;
he rescues those who are crushed in spirit.
—Psalm 34:18 (New Living Translation)

Lord,
you know what's going on here.
You know where I'm confused
and where I hurt
and what I'm questioning,
and what I'm wondering about.

I'm a captive to my past,
captive to my fears,
captive to my false sense of security,
captive to my pride and my judgmentalism and my petty demands.

You know about all the times
I've failed to let your Spirit blow
through my life.

I feed on emptiness until I'm stuffed,
and then I wonder why you seem so distant.

From all of these chains there is freedom;
from all of these cages, a key.
Release me.
Reveal yourself.
And set me free.

death was conquered on a cross,
life was born in a tomb.
how's that for turning the tables
on destiny?

To the architect of the infinite.

A reason to serve you?
You are the king.

A reason to trust you?
You are the truth.

A reason to worship?
You are the mystery.

A reason to die?
You are the life.

A reason to follow?
You are the path.

A reason to get out of bed
and face the morning?
The empty tomb.

Listen to me inside,
under my words
where the shivering is.
—from *Guerrillas of Grace*
by Ted Loder

Bread of Life,
You are full of promises;
I've heard them echo deep within me:
longings and dreams for a better day, a brighter day.
This world, stunning though it is,
doesn't satisfy the part of me
that's the most hungry.

Eternity calls to me,
transcendence tugs at me,
and wonder whispers to me
whenever I hear your story.

I have a nagging thirst for more
than this world can provide.

Deepen it.

Free all the heavenly longings
encased in the stony prison of
my heart.

you are the wonder of spirit and flesh,
the story of an infant divine.
for a God without blood could never enmesh
a soul as blemished as mine.

To you.

Majesty,
Mystery,
Love and Desire,
Terror through History,
Wonder and Fire.
    Grace for the outcast,
    balm for my sorrow,
    dreams wrapped in heartache,
hope for tomorrow.

Listening,
following
voice in the night,
Poet of Wonder,
Call to Delight.
    Peace for the prodigal,
    homecoming feast,
    wedding for prostitutes,
love for the least.

Lamb of Eternity
Carpenter Bard,
Rebel to All Who Are
Trying too Hard.
    Revealer of hypocrites,
    peace to the sea,
    madman from Nazareth,
brother to me.

the purest form of humility
is to no longer be concerned about humility.

Breath of Life, breathe on me.
Wind of God, blow through me.
Spirit of Truth, rebirth me.
Pull back the covers of my practical, logical world and baptize my knowledge with the mystery of faith.

Help me to believe and to stop trying to understand,
after all, how could I ever wrap my mind around something—
Someone—
greater than the universe itself?

Convert my imagination
just as much as you have informed my intellect.
Your presence doesn't make me comfortable,
but it comforts me.
Your light isn't easy to look at,
but it reveals me.

The spiritual life is an absurd mystery.
Help me to enter it,
as it enters me.
The first step isn't one of reason, but of faith.

I lift my foot.

there are gifts
that only a teardrop and a raindrop
and a summer meadow bring,
and you created them all.

To the one who gives life,
and is life.

You tell me to pick up my cross
and to lay down my burdens—
why do you speak in riddles about
something as important as my pain?

Is it true that the only way to find life
is by passing through the doorway of suffering?
Why does the road to life
have to lead directly to the cross?
I wish it led straight from the garden to the empty
tomb.

If I'm ever going to walk in your paths,
I need you to show me how to lay down the
burden of my past,
and pick up the beams of freedom—
I don't know how to do it on my own.

Your grace has arms strong enough
to carry all that I bear,
and to lift me when I stumble
beneath the weight of loving you.

over the years so many folds
have creased the fabric of my heart—
unwrinkle me.

Seeking Savior,
Loving Father,
Living Comforter,
sometimes the simplest admissions are the best:

I'm holding a grudge and I like it
and I need you to help me let go of it
or I never will.

I keep comparing myself to others and I know it's stupid
but I do it anyway.

I tend to base my feelings of self-worth
on what I have and on how much I accomplish,
rather than on how much I matter to you.

I'm so angry right now, that I feel like killing someone.
I'm disappointed with the people around me
and enjoy telling them so.
I want to look at porn, I'm sorry.

I'm still feeling guilty about my abortion
and I don't think I'm ever going to get over it.
I feel my faith slipping and you don't seem
real to me anymore.

I'm frustrated.
I'm confused.
I'm feeling sorry for myself again.

I need you.
Don't abandon me.
I'm reaching out to you,
have mercy on me.

fill the silence of my heart
with words that disturb me
enough to finally
bring me
peace.

To the one who speaks from the storm.

When you confronted Job
and showed him his smallness,
he placed his hand over his mouth.

What more is there to say?
You are God.
I am me.
Silence is the only response
eloquent enough to acknowledge
who you truly are.

Watch over us who are still in our dangerous voyage.
—a prayer of St. Augustine

Lord,
the river ripples before me,
promising new shores.

I feel the pull of the current,
  the welcoming immersion,
but I've been clinging
to this rotting stump
for as long as I can remember,
  and now I can't seem to let go.

Be gracious enough
to tug me beneath the surface.

mystics can find a lifetime
of inspiration in a grain of sand.
for the rest of us it takes at least a mountain.

Spirit of Truth and Glory,
let dewdrop and blossom,
teardrop and scream,
    flame and frost and angry sky,
bring you praise, shout your name.

Let tiger and turtle and guppy,
let laughter and barley and sand
adore your unspeakable name.

Let all the earth praise the Lord—
    mountains and minnows and molecules,
    boulders and falcons and toads.
Let the sky praise the Lord—
    thunderclouds, rainbows and steel blue horizons,
    twilight and midnight and equatorial sun.

And now let the nighttime sing!
And now let the comets shout!
And now let the galaxies rollick with praise!

Then pry open the space between the natural
and the supernatural,
and let me join the song
that's been ringing since
the beginning of time.

mostly i sit so far from the flame
that i can still feel the chill of the night.

create a blaze bright enough to finally
give me blisters.

Comfort spoke to me.

"I'm a gentle goddess," she said. "I would never ask to control you. I only want to set you free. Isn't that what you want? What all men want? The end of the struggle and the beginning of ease?"

And I had to agree with her. Most of my dreams and my plans and my choices were rooted in the desire for more comfort or convenience.

"I'm not like other gods," she said. "I'm not like the gods of anger or justice or mercy or jealousy. I make no demands of you. I require no service of you. No worship. No fire. I serve you, instead."

The words of Comfort stirred me and moved me toward myself with their enticements.

"I'm an easy goddess to honor. Some gods try to wake you up with conviction or conversion or contrition, but I'm most satisfied when you're asleep in my arms. Don't ask yourself what I might desire, but only what you would desire of me. For I give you my all. And I'm here to fulfill your wildest desires, not just meet your needs."

Comfort reached her hand to me and I took it. For she was lovely to behold and her smile encircled my heart. We moved toward each other in a lover's embrace.

"Lean on me," she said. "Come to me. Set down your cross and take my hand. My road is easy and the path is smooth and every step is more relief from the harsh load of other gods."

She led me to her chambers.

"Throw away your yokes, for I seek to remove them one and all. And in your dreams, don't think of other worlds, but of this one. You deserve all that this moment can offer, all that I can give. I'll shield you from suffering, shut out pain, and protect you from any cruel thoughts of grief or death."

I smelled her perfume as she leaned her body against mine. Then Comfort guided me toward her bed. And our lips met and I found in her kisses the soothing and unhurried promises of ease.

"I'm a pillow for your head and shoes for your feet and gloves for your hands. I protect you and soothe you as you move from one moment to the next. I whisper to you; hear my voice! I'm the goddess of today and the moments within it. And I gently cradle all my children, singing them to sleep in my arms."

And that's when I saw the chains hanging from her wrists and the shackles hidden in her bed.

So I ran from her. I fled from her and limped away from her side. And since that night I have been careful not to return to her arms.

Yet, my heart is still pounding with desire. And her perfume still lingers on my lips.

you loved me so much that you put skin on your story,
and then poured your story into my skin.

To the ancient and future king.

You are the one who shapes
the interplay of space and time,
but still finds a way
to lend your attention
    to me.

Your fingers formed the planets
and sent them pinballing into space.
Your lips blew spirit-life
into Adam's cold and lonely clay.
Your eyes have seen the future
and searched a trillion hearts;
    and you waited three days sleeping
    on the sidewalks of Jerusalem,
hoping your mother would remember
who you really were.
And now I see you waiting just as patiently
for me to do the same.

This is how I would die
into the love I have for you:
as pieces of cloud
dissolve in sunlight.
—from the *Soul of Rumi*,
edited by Coleman Barks

To the one who is honest and true.

I have become an expert
at playing the role
of someone who's got his act together.

I'm tired of all the acting, though,
all the false smiles and familiar façades.

Open the eyes of my friends
so that they can see the real me;
and help me
help them
by seeing past all the self-contained glances
to the real person inside.

You came to be the great unmasker.
Unmask us all.

you accept the music of my life
even though it is only clanging noise
to the rest of the world.

To the one who knows me as I really am and still loves me.

Today, I bring all of me—
my hopes and my fears,
my dreams and my doubts;
the part of me that likes to please other people
and the part that genuinely desires you.

I bring all of me—
my anger and my past,
my goals and my priorities,
my flagrant forgetfulness of your glory,
and the familiar memories of my pain.

Here are my loves,
here are my needs,
here is my hurt,
here is my desire.

I bring my gifts as well.
All that I have and all that I am—
the abilities you gave me,
the training I've acquired,
the motivation to do good,
the strength of my convictions,
the influence I have with others,
the interests and passions that inspire me.

I bring you my stuff—
so much stuff, that I've cluttered
my heart and my home with.
I bring you my stuff as well.

I bring all of me—
my relationships and my needs,
my sins and my pride and my portfolio.

My checkbook,
calendar,
wallet,
credit cards,
schedule,
time off,
time at work.

My all—
my eyes and the things I look at,
my tongue and the words I say,
my ears and my hands and my feet,
my heart and my mind and my soul,
    and my will.

The cursing part,
the complacent part,
the depressed part,
the apathetic part,
the lazy, lonely, misguided, power-hungry me.
I bring you my all.

I bring you myself.

Even the hesitation I have to pray this prayer,
even the pride that I have for praying it,
even the fear that you might actually take me
    seriously
    and expect all of this from me.
Even those things.
I bring them all
and offer them
to you here, today.

—furious love—
is that why you stepped
onto the page of this world
with a whip in one hand,
and a chalice in the other?

To the God who answers prayer.

Every tear I shed
gives birth to another piece of the enigma.
Life is a puzzling mixture
of pain and glory, of delight and despair.
I tend to retreat from the extremes,
into my preciously guarded middle-class cocoon,
  my middle-class blindness,
  my middle-class life.
I need to hear the wails again,
the deep and ever-present cry of our dying world.

And also, I need to hear the giggles again
of my childlike God playing in the sand,
calling me to start the honest journey
into the troubling paradox of faith.

you created us and we gave birth to you.
what kind of God lets his children
play with such dangerous joy?

Patient Groom,
your love fills me with a strange kind of emptiness,
and your longing for me fills me
    with longing for you.

How can I be so empty and yet so full,
so alive and yet so dead?

Can springtime and winter
really live in the same moment,
bloom in the same heart?

I hear snatches of your song,
I catch glimpses of your beauty,
I sense echoes of your strength
    reverberating through this hurting world.

Thank you for these gentle reminders
that you are here,
and that you are working
in the enigma of who I am,
to shape me daily
into the person I was always meant
    to become.

i set down the moment i was carrying
so that i could bicker with my friend about oblivion,
and when i reached down to pick it up
it was gone.

that's the story of my life in a nutshell.

To you.

I like to strive for perfection,
and forget that it will always be elusive
and deceptive.

But since you arose,
the pressure of performance is over.

Now I can stop this mad and frantic game
and simply receive the illumination,
the presence,
the relationship that
is always available right here in this present,
fleeting moment.

Help me to avoid pandering to accolades and
applause,
and willingly disappear
into you instead.

i know that you are the author of my faith.
now, be the editor.

Lion, Lamb, Lover, Lord,
when I'm tempted to anchor myself in quicksand,
    restrain me.
When I'm tempted to wander into my own
private red-light district,
    redirect me.
When I'm tempted to start believing
that I really am the person I portray to others,
    reveal me,
both to myself and to them.

Help me to know, more and more,
what it means to not only live with you,
    but within you;
to not only live for you,
    but lean toward you.

Help me escape the siren call of this world,
    that leads only toward the rocks,
and instead, help me find a new vision
that leads closer to you.

O master poet, I have sat down at thy feet. Only let me make my life simple and straight, like a flute of reed for thee to fill with music.
—from *Gitanjali* by Rabindranath Tagore

All-knowing Creator,
why do you paint rainbows among the mists
of the rocky shores and grow stalactites
deep in the unexplored caves?

Why do you wed yourself to a beauty
that goes so utterly unnoticed?
Unwelcomed?
Unseen?

Why do you take such care
in shaping a billion snowflakes, one by one,
to fall on the arctic lands?
    Why, when so many melt unseen?
Why do you weave sunlight
into the fabric of the towering forests
    so that it can frolic
    without an audience
    in the shade of the sequoias?

Is it a game that you play to pass the time,
or are you so enamored with beauty
that you can't help but spread it
lavishingly into all the corners
of the universe you love?

my heart is a gordian knot.
i've tried to untie it and failed.

be alexander the great to me,
slice through the deep
and tangled cordage
of my past.

So God,
I cry out to you,
and you ignore me.
I lean on you,
and you let me fall on my face.
I trust in you,
and you don't come through for me.
You keep hurting me.
Why?

What kind of a God are you anyway?
Prayer is supposed to help, right?
You're supposed to be listening
to me, answering me, helping me,
but all you give me is silence.

Where are you?

I can't believe how much I've trusted you,
and how many times you've let me down.

I feel betrayed.
Don't let this go on any longer.
If you're there, help me.
I need you and I can't stand
feeling abandoned any longer.

all of my love is stained with myself.
all of your love is washed
with blood.

A prayer to the one who taught us to pray.

When I actually take the time to look,
I see you've formed thousands of deep rivers
in the hidden canyons of my soul.
  But for some reason, when I approach you,
I so often dip my prayers from
such shallow, muddy pools instead.

Today, I drop all the religious-sounding platitudes,
the inane repetitions,
and the safe, comfortable shiny prayers
that I typically offer you.

Today I bring you
the rough-cut boulders of my heart.

Here are my nagging questions,
my disquieting loves,
my troubling secrets,
and my very human needs.
I give them all to you today,
no holding back,
no playing it safe.

Here are my unfulfilled longings,
my unmet demands,
my deeply rooted disappointments,
and the things I fear but pretend to control.

Here, for you, O Savior,
I offer my unquenchable worship.
my wordless groans,
my deepest needs.

No more veneer.

Simply thoughts of pain,
of regret,
of hope,
of you.

Today, I give you the rushing,
tumbling waters of myself.

something ancient stirs
within my chest. i hear a scream as wild as night,
and as soft as daisies:
  you are alive, child.
  you are alive.
  you are part of the unfolding day.

slowly i open my eyes
to a new kind of dawn.

Lamb of God,
Lion of the Ages,
too often I remember lessons,
but forget your tale.

I forget the sound of Egyptian mothers
  screaming in the night,
the hot sweat on the foreheads of your children in the
  desert,
and the sting of the viper's bite on my leg.

I forget the taste of the fruit on my lips,
the terror of seeing your cloud of glory, and the
ache in the heart of your prophets
  as they waited in vain for you
  and died without seeing your promises come true.

I flip the page in my Bible
from the Old Testament to the New
and forget all the years that passed
with the words, "I will send a curse"
echoing in the minds of your people.

I forget the dew on the feet of the women who
walked the dawn-lit trail to your tomb;
and I forget the whisper of heaven,
the scent of new life,
the feel of your scars beneath my fingers,
the tremble of virgin hope being born.

I forget these things and when I do,
the tale dissolves and the mystery and glory fade
away.

Help me to remember your story
and to step inside it again.

Remember, Lord, that men are apt to make slips;
we are a spineless race, given to blundering:
think of our build, our limitations.
Our skins may be sound,
but there are sores underneath.

—a prayer found on a fourth century
Egyptian papyrus (from *Every Eye Beholds*
You, edited by Thomas J. Craughwell)

To the giver of freedom and fullness.

The closer I inspect my heart,
the more holes I find
hidden
beneath my reputation and
my respectable, upstanding life.

So many holes.

And I've tried to fill them in so many ways:
workaholism and masturbation,
the subtle pride of the comparison game,
self-indulgence and sports and
wise career moves.
I've done the bigger-house-better-car-wiser-
investments thing.
I've tried to drown my sorrow in liquid heartache,
and sweet, sweet easy-to-swallow pills.

And despite what people say,
all of those things do work,
  not at healing the emptiness,
  but as useful distractions.

Some people actually succeed in making
it through their whole lives without ever living,
just constantly covering the holes
with things that eventually tip into them.

What I need is fewer distractions
not more.

So here is my potholed heart,
I offer it to you.
  Empty out the emptiness,
fill me with your fullness,
and when I try pursuing those
glistening diversions
sting me with regret
as your way of showing you care.

it's easy for me to mock
idols of wood and stone
because mine are so much more
commercially viable and technologically advanced.

To the sower.

I feel the thorns choking me
the birds robbing me,
the sun scorching me.

The evil one's talons sink in,
suffering drains my resolve,
worry overwhelms me,
riches impress me,
    and pleasures distract me.
I am three tragic soils in one.

Untangle me,
uproot the thorns in my life.
cultivate the soil of my heart,
for I'm so quickly ensnared,
so easily entangled
    in the many alluring brambles of this world.

The dark soil whispers to my soul,
so give me an undivided heart,

that I might fear your name,
walk in your truth,
and produce a crop that lasts.

Mercy.
Have mercy on me,
and let my roots
grow deeper into
kingdom soil.

the great mystery:
you chose to step into our story.

the great tragedy:
we killed you for caring so much.

Comforter,
reach down with your mercy,
the night stretches before me,
the pain is so deep.

I feel the scars of my past
spreading across today.
Wrap me in your might,
pierce me with your glory,
startle me with your
  unsettling love.

at times i thought
he was a villain in a
hero's disguise.
but after i saw him cry,
i realized it was
the other way around.

Lord,
take my anger and beat it to pieces.

Drive disobedience from my heart.
Use the strongest whip you own.
Let your love be merciless in me;
it's the only way to conquer a heart
as rebellious as mine.

Slay my anger
and leave me vacant enough
to be filled with you.

Even now I'm lowering the fists of my heart
in surrender.

the sting of glory is too
bright for my
tender earth-eyes to see.

thank you for stepping
behind the veil.

To the Christ.

What kind of love is this?
A love so pure and perfect
that it cannot help but die for its beloved.
A love so everlasting
  that eternity is swallowed up in its wings.
A love so unfailing
  that it remains faithful through a thousand
  betrayals.
A love so tender
  that it washes away the tears of the world.
A love so powerful
  that it breaks the teeth of death
  and conquers all the powers of darkness.

You suffered and the world laughed;
you died and everyone went back to work.
You rose and now my moments matter
at last.

whenever you enter my heart
i hear the sound of a temple
curtain ripping
in half.

A prayer to the living God.

Let me be as faithful as the wind,
as radiant as the sun,
as blameless as the stars,
as pure as the sea.

Here is my heart, help me to become
as brave as the sky,
as humble as the meadow,
as cheerful as the dawn,
as bold as the mountains.

Today let me rise praising you,
speak praising you,
love praising you,
sleep praising you,
    breathe, think, dream, live
    praising you.

Glory calls to me,
creation welcomes me,
wonder whispers my name,
and I can't help but reply.

i'm not sure whether to
ask you to soften the path
or to cover it with
sharper thorns
so that i'll finally leave it
and follow
yours.

God,
when I first started this journey
I expected the rain of your
presence to be gentle,
but when I stepped into the storm
I found that every drop was both freezing
and somehow
laced with fire.

Baptisms don't come easily
to wayward souls
like mine.

we inherit that which
we value most:
intimacy with you,
or eternity with ourselves.

O All-Knowing King,
at the feast that you serve,
children dance in the courtyard
but the wolf still prowls the woodlands
here around my home.

The breadcrumbs have been snatched away
by the ravens I released
into the forest last year.

Never before has the witch's brew
tasted so good,
never before has the spell-mist around me
been so thick.

I am lost, so lost
in the dark wood.

I hear the king calling for me
to join him in the castle.

Come find me.
Please.

Take the sharp blade of your tale
and slice through my forgetting.
Sweep me up in your story,
and let the truest myth of all
become everything to me.

every moment
you speak a thousand sunrises
into my night.
why do i find it so hard
to say thank you?

To you.

O, Light Above the Darkness,
Truth Above the Lies,
Ruler of the Galaxies,
King Above the Skies,
Mystery of Ages,
Wonder of the Tale,
  calm me in the tempest,
  guide me through the gale.

Lover of the Wanderer,
Prince of Those Who Stray,
I bow before your majesty,
  rule in me today.

a moment ago a child was born.
—celebrate—
another professor has come
to teach us about the kingdom.

God of the Dawn and the Day,
let me be young enough to kiss your elbow
and believe in fairies and dragons.

Let me be young enough to run, not walk, toward the
    playground,
and when I fall, to just get back up again,
and when other kids cry, to join them and not
be ashamed.

Let me be young enough to make snow angels
and climb trees in the twilight—
to be frightened of the darkness
and unwilling to stay in the big house all alone,
and astonished by dandelions
    and quick to chase fireflies.

Let me be young enough to believe, really believe,
that you rose from the dead
and live in my heart,
    and then, make me so excited about it
that I can't help but tell
all the other kids at recess that God actually
lives inside of me.

Let me be young enough to be afraid of
what's going to happen to me when
Dad gets home, but humble enough
to run to him and cling to his leg when he does.

Let me be young enough to spill my ice cream
and then presumptuous enough to ask for more;
young enough to say my prayers
and trust that they'll be heard.

Let me be young enough
to bring you my stick-figure drawings
and know that you'll find room for them on your
fridge.

Let me become child enough
to step through the door to your kingdom
and then realize, in one astonishing
moment of somersault excitement,
that heaven is more like a sleepover
than an elders' meeting,
more like eating macaroni and cheese with Dad
or playing in the tree house
than sitting through a Sunday morning
church service.

Because then, when I'm finally that young,
I'll finally be born.

all the syllables of my story
were covered with dust and dead tears
until you began to whisper the words.

O Living Wonder,
your clouds catch the sunlight
and juggle it through the day.

The mountains bow before you.
Glory, Glory is your name.

I feel the weight that lifts all burdens;
the terror that softens my soul.

You surround me with the aroma of heaven,
and I praise you for letting me experience its
fragrance.

This promise, this assurance
of something to look forward to,
defines me backward through time,
drawing me home.

I praise you.
I am part of creation, part of your
endless dream.

We've all become unclean,
and all our righteous acts
are like permanently stained rags.
—Isaiah 64:6

Holy One,
Pure One,
keep me from the soul-deadening goal
of trying to be good.

Protect me from the traps of niceness and fame
and draw me closer to the brutal truth
of my fallenness.
Let my politeness fall away,
and sear my good intentions.
Burn them to a crisp.

Slay my compromise,
my political correctness,
my tactful but artificial niceties.

Destroy the foolhardy aspirations I have of becoming a good person;
let me be a soul-grieved, awe-inspired follower of you;
a kingdom-child who is being daily washed clean and pure
by your undeserved love and favor.

Grace is a reality.
And it is more than I could ever ask.

the wine in my heart is stale.
empty it out;
and pour in your Son's blood.

after all, i hear they're
almost the same thing.

O Jesus,
I've been an orphan so long
that when you invited me to join your family
I was afraid to leave the orphanage.

For some reason, I like to hold
onto my pain.
I know it doesn't make sense,
but maybe it's because
guilt is so familiar to me,
maybe that's why I don't want to let it go.

So often I'm tempted to retreat into my shame.
It feels familiar and necessary somehow—
a great, grievous, crushing companion.
It's so hard to set it down, to leave it behind.
I think that at times I even get some kind of
reassurance,
even pleasure, from feeling bad
about my past.

I clench the darkness so fervently.
Loosen my grip
and let the sweet and airy
freedom of grace lift me
from myself.

i cannot
undo the act,
but i can let you
untie the shame.

Father,
I know you said, "Have no other gods before me,"
but what about other goals?
Do those count?

(OK, I admit I'm looking for a little wiggle room here between your expectations and my desires, but it sure would be nice to have some kind of ammunition, or at least a little place to hide when you come knocking.)

"Child,
goals can become gods
as easily as life can become busy.
My commands are also invitations
to the richest life possible."

Then, please,
be the only goal
the only reason,
the only agenda I have.

I choose you.

Pierce this moment with your presence.
Pervade my heart and fill my days.
Open every corner of my life to you.
Saturate my goals,
my priorities, my agendas,
with yourself until all of them match yours.

you call us into this curious place
of remembering grace
and forgetting pain,
and here i am again,
doing the opposite.

O Waker of the Dead,
awaken me.

Find the faith in my soul that's as dead as night;
find the hope in my heart that's as dry as dust;
find the love in my spirit that's so fast asleep.
  Peer beneath the shroud of my life
and awaken me.

Look deeply, Jesus.
  Find the child there,
  find the dreamer there,
  find the lover there.
Awaken me.

You're the one who has conquered the grave,
you're the one who has tasted new life.
Help me die to the dying life,
  and be born to the life that never dies,
by entering the mystery of your love
right here,
right now, today.

o poet king,
forgive me for bothering
you earlier today.
  i didn't know my life stanza
was already written on your hand.

To the one who deserves my allegiance.

Here's something that's hard for me to remember:
the God who is,
  is.
And that means you're right here, right now.

And you were there in sixth grade
  when I got into that fight,
and in eighth grade
  when those kids were making fun of me,
and in high school
  when I felt so lonely and lost, like I didn't fit in.
All along, you were there.

All along.

Remind me that I'm never alone,
and that, because of your glorious return,
I never will be.

narrow vision and flavorless moments
have become my home.
the feast of awakening begins the moment i open my
eyes.

Compassionate One,
sometimes I get tired of all the competing
for jobs and attention and parking spaces and love.
People say it's a dog-eat-dog world,
and it's me against them,
and it's a jungle out there.
and it's a rat race
and life isn't easy, you know, so you
just have to grin and bear it.

And I guess in certain ways all those things are true,
but not as true as they seem.

I'd rather not have to grin and bear it
since you already bore it all
and while you did, you didn't grin,
you wept.

And you still do.

You weep because of
the bookmarked porn,
and the middle-class envy,
and the lives bound in materialism,
and the secret little grudges we hold on to
but pretend we don't,
and the church traditions that strangle
the free spontaneity of your Spirit.

You weep because we're living the dog-eat-dog
us-against-them

jungle-out-there-rat-race life,
and you designed us for something
so much more magnificent.

Here's my desire:
that I stop pursuing such tragic distractions;
    stop clawing and worrying and hurrying
and instead,
simply receive all that this moment has to offer.
That is my desire.
That is my prayer.

So here are my burdens,
my worries,
my fears and regrets.
I'm ready to stop running
    the race of the rats
and start walking the kingdom path.

Eternity is a seed of fire whose sudden roots
break barriers that keep my heart from being an abyss.
—from *Dialogues with Silence* by Thomas Merton

Lord,
make my sin as loathsome to me as it is to you,
    and drown my ambition
in the sea of your will.

If my sadness could be weighed and my troubles be put on the scales, they would be heavier than all the sands of the sea.

—Job 6:2–3 (New Living Translation)

To the one who is supposed to care.

You seem so far away.
  So distant,
So indifferent to my prayers
and my needs.

Why do you let the guilty go unpunished,
and the innocent get imprisoned?

Why do you allow genocide and racism
and murder and torture and rape?

When I cry out to you,
why don't you make yourself more visible,
  more tangible to me?
Why are you so silent?

When my friends need me, I don't abandon them.
When my friends bring me their problems
  I do all I can to help them.
But that's not how you treat me.

You beat me up when I'm down
and ignore me when I'm hurting.

What kind of a God treats his children like that?
What kind of God are you, anyway?

innocence is a place my soul
walked away from a long time ago.
and yet, by your strange grace,
it is also my new forwarding address.

Mysterious One,
take me by surprise.

A normal day and a
normal yawn and then I feel your
Spirit passing across my shadow.
A flash of reassurance,
a sudden realization that you delight in me.
You, the star-speaking poet,
you, the dragon-slaying prince,
you, the battle-scarred carpenter,
actually take delight in me.

You actually do.

So now, at last,
I accept the invitation
to take delight
in you.

my inward-facing eyeballs
scour my heart for more reasons to feel important.
and always find more than enough.

Judge and Advocate,
I don't really understand what people mean
when they talk about forgiving themselves.

Forgiveness means canceling a debt.

So, if I hurt others, they can forgive me;
if I hurt you, you can forgive me.
But how can I cancel the debt I owe another person?

Today, rather than trying to forgive myself,
—which all too often means
simply excusing myself
or ignoring the seriousness of my offenses—
help me to do the harder thing,
and accept the full and free forgiveness you offer.

I know this will take more courage
and honesty and humility
than I have on my own.

Be gracious enough
to draw me into the place
where I can finally say yes to you,
and receive the forgiveness that accepts no excuses,
and keeps no tally,
and asks only faith,
and offers ultimate freedom
in return.

the same stars that
watched over you, watch over
me as i step across the soft
arc of the earth.

God of All Galaxies,
Speaker of the Stars,
the temple of the sky shows your glory,
the temples of the mountains speak your name,
the temple of the sea reveals your peace—
    and your rage.
And the temple of my heart knows your
troublesome grace.

The temple of my home
gives me the chance to love you
    by loving others,
The temple of my car
gives me the chance to pray for the residents
    of every house I pass.
The temple of my work
gives me the chance to offer you
    daily sacrifices disguised as proposals,
emails, meetings, service calls, grunt work
and inboxes.

I have more than enough temples in my life.
So why do I offer you such little worship?

you are the remedy;
unpoison my past.

To the bringer of freedom
and allower of pain.

We both know what happened there,
a little while back.

It wasn't that I wanted to turn my back on you,
it didn't happen all at once.
It was so gradual that I didn't even notice
I was turning away
until I couldn't see you beside me at all.

And then.
Well.
We both know what I did.

Wrap me in grace.
Unwind the pain that crushes my joy.
I need you,
I cry out to you.

Forgive me.
I love you,
and I'm sorry.

i am a dot on the fabric of the universe,
yet you choose to notice me.

my heart swells
and I burst at the thought.

O Jesus, your life rhymes with love.
Your miracles touched
  the divine.
You are the carpenter of hearts,
power of life,
beloved groom of harlot souls,
light of the universe,
spinner of tales,
with glory greater than any star,
and enough humility
to wash your disciples' feet.

You share sunlight and hope,
you offer mercy and acceptance,
and give love and forgiveness,
in an unending, undiminishing
supply.

You are able,
I am willing.
Quiet me again.

My soul reaches out
its trembling finger
to touch your hand,
but I can't find it,
  because it's already on my shoulder
guiding me home.

i turn my back to the mirror
and tell myself i'm ok.

and i find it's much easier
to convince myself when
i'm not looking at my reflection.

The Angel of the Lord appeared to me and said, "The Lord is waiting."

Apparently we had an appointment today,
and it must have slipped my mind because
I can't find it anywhere on my calendar.

"That's odd," I said. "I don't remember scheduling a meeting."

"That's because you're not the one who did," said the Angel of the Lord.

i say "yes" to myself,
and the aroma of shame
sinks deeper into the pit
of who i am.

i say "yes" to you
and your Spirit clears the air.

God,
my life gets so easily skewed,
so quickly unbalanced;
with so many messy relationships,
and pressing deadlines,
and dueling obligations.

All too often, everything in me
that seems to be on-target
    and on-track
gets thrown out-of-whack.

Yet, all the while,
you offer a different kind of hope.
One that renews me even in the day-to-day world
of shopping lists
and dirty laundry
and hangnails
and cold sores.

Wonder reaches out to me,
but the dailiness of life bats it away.
Let glory sweep over me again.

daylight dims
but your light never fades,
O Ever-Present Dawn.

To the one I adore.

There's a hymn that asks you
for a thousand tongues to sing your praise.
For me, one tongue is enough.
I don't dare pray for a thousand,
I'm having trouble enough taming the one I have.

My mutinous tongue
so often drips poison
    instead of lifting praise.

Instead of a thousand tongues,
let me bring you one,
just one,
that is actually,
    honestly,
unashamedly,
wholeheartedly,
singing your praise.

Then after I get that down,
we can move on from there.

we live sweaty, reeking, desperate little lives,
but have dreams of paradise and eternity.

we are the enigma positioned graciously
between the angels and the apes.

O Everlasting God,
my heart is torn between where I've been
and where I'm going,
where I am and where I want to be,
what I dream of,
and what I see happening in my life.

I'm torn
between my will and yours,
between my responsibilities
and my desires,
between the life you ask of me
and the life
I demand from you.

Sometimes I think I'm the only one walking this journey,
of lostness and foundness,
of being both the bride and the prostitute,
the pirate and the priest,
the beggar and the child of the king,
wandering and wondering my way through
the questions.

You became the path
for all who are willing
to walk away from the confusion.

I offer you my next step,
let my foot land beside yours.

help me, O God,
climb above myself.

Spirit,
Creator
Savior,
I pray so many
wormy, mealy, glib little prayers,
  banal and tepid and dry.
So today, instead, I will ask mighty things—
supernatural things,
wonderful things that seem too good
and too big to come true.

"You do not have because you do not ask,"
you said.

And so, now I ask
for peace between Israel and its neighbors,
and the end of violence in Africa,
and the disruption of terrorist plans.

I pray for healing
to those suffering from earthquakes and fires,
from hurricanes and tornadoes,
from flooding and drought and famine,
and for more loving families
  willing to adopt the lonely orphans of the world.

Bring
comfort to the dying,
selflessness to the rich,
courage to fathers to stay with their families
and patience for mothers to nurture their children.

I ask you to change hearts and laws
so that the story of your love can be taken
to countries where your followers are persecuted,
    so that the lost might be found,
    the hopeless might discover a reason for living
    and the lonely their true place in your family.

Inspire more justice for the underprivileged,
more compassion for the land,
more programs that help the poor
    rather than pad the wallets of the rich.

I pray for those living in ghettos and grottos,
that you would open doors of hope and opportunity,
and that you would inspire the children
to lean toward new dreams and possibilities
    instead of comfortable violence.

Punish those
who abuse and rape children.

Heal the hearts of those
who struggle with
despair and depression,
who are caught in marriages in crisis,
or drowning in debt,
or suffering from grief or loss or anger.
    Heal their hurting hearts.

Give me the courage to offer you prayers
as big as your power and your love.

stagnant waters
never produce
healthy fish.

ripple my sea.

Father,
from now on as we talk,
I'll be sharing more of my life with you,
as well as the stuff that frustrates me,
the things I'm concerned about,
and where I'm hurting,
and what I'm hoping for,
and thinking about,
and planning,
and remembering,
and sometimes, if you don't mind,
I'd like to just sit with you
and not say anything at all.

Sound OK to you?

cure me of the most deadly and subtle of all addictions: the infatuation with doing things my way.

A parable.

The disciple went to the temple and laid his life before his Lord. Filled with reverence and awe, he bowed before the altar.

And a voice thundered from the sanctuary, "Leave this place. Leave me. You are no follower of mine."

"But Lord," cried the disciple, "I have been your follower for all these years. I've given to your work, I've abstained from impure thoughts and recited all the prayers that the elders taught me to pray."

"You can't worship me until you know me. And you can't know me until you love me. And you can't love me until you've learned to hate yourself."

"Hate? You want me to hate?" the man said. "No, I will not. There's no room for hatred in my religion. You aren't my god after all."

And then he rose and brushed himself off and went away to find a new Lord to worship.

One that made a little more sense.

You must stop examining spiritual truths like dry bones! You must break open the bones and take in the life-giving marrow.

—from the *Wisdom of the Sadhu*,
edited by Kim Comer

Jesus,
I know it's not politically correct to talk about hell
and that many well-meaning, faithful people
believe it exists,
and many others don't believe in it at all.

Well, you know where I stand on the whole issue,
and today I ask that my beliefs
would become more like yours.

Carpenter Rabbi,
in your stories, your parables,
you made it clear that those who follow you
will end up in a place of excitement,
    celebration and community,
but everyone who follows his own agenda instead,
will eventually arrive at a place of fierce
    loneliness, regret and despair.

Let those two simple truths
guide me through this day—
    my way leads to despair,
    your way leads to celebration.
Shape my choices
and bridle my tongue and my heart
in whatever ways necessary
to keep me walking on the kingdom path,
instead of the road toward myself.

everywhere i look, i see reasons to laugh,
and reasons to weep,
so how do i manage to go so long
without doing either?

To the revealer of souls.

If you're alive,
then the everyday,
in-your-face,
dragged-through-the-dirt,
stabbed-in-the-back,
hung-out-to-dry world
  has a point,
and my worrisome little moments
woven together with fear and disgrace
  have meaning.

If you're really there,
then the winds of change have blown,
and the gifts of the future
touch the here and the now.

It's easy to focus on the drudgery of life,
but if you're real, every moment is
exquisitely rich and
filled with possibility.

And you are alive,
  so, this moment matters
for all eternity.

if i can't find the strength to
shout my hallelujah,
maybe someday i'll find the courage
to whisper it.

To the God who pursues.

Our world is groaning around me
and my heart groans with it.

So many tears and questions,
so many stillborn children,
so much cancer and divorce,
so many orphans and so much poverty.
Closing my eyes doesn't make
the wailing stop;
doesn't turn the grief into joy.

I hear your Spirit groaning with me,
taking the cry of my heart to your throne.
Hear our groans.
Have mercy on us.

australia began as a land of convicts
and became an island of surfers.
that's the kind of transformation i need.
let the waves roll in.

Patient One,
sometimes it seems like the past
has a stranglehold on today.

The harsh words I've said
and the petty grudges I've held
and the frustrated sighs I've let out,
somehow reach up through time
and wrap their coarse fingers around my throat.
And squeeze.

Is it true that mercy is unlimited?
that compassion is new every day?
that every dawning moment offers
a second second-chance?

Unwrap the grip of the past
and let the call of the future
lead me home.

We run carelessly to the precipice, after we have put something before us to prevent us seeing it.

—from *Pensées* by Blaise Pascal,
seventeenth century philosopher
and mathematician

A parable.

"Oh, wise Teacher!" called the students. "Speak to us of Temptation!"

"What do you know of it already?" he asked.

"I know it's like an avalanche," said one of the students. "Starting with only a small snowflake and burying the person in cold death."

"Some temptation," said the Teacher. "But not all."

"Then it is a piece of driftwood caught in a current. And the driftwood doesn't notice it's moving at all until it has been carried far downstream," said another student.

"Yes, that is true of some temptation. But only of some."

"But what of all temptation?" they cried.

"All temptation looks as the rose, with promises sweet and fragrant, and they are beautiful to touch, but once plucked, the thorns on the stem wound the picker of the rose. Yet every day, the person returns to pick another rose, and is wounded once again by its thorns."

"But why would the person not stop picking roses?" asked the students.

"Because the rose remains beautiful, even through the pain," said the Teacher.

O waiting soul, be still, be strong,
And though He tarry, trust and wait;
Doubt not, He will not wait too long,
Fear not, He will not come too late.
—from *Streams in the Desert*

Gracious One,
I'm tempted to let Christianity become
something I talk about—
like the weather,
or the ball game,
or the upcoming election,
rather than a life-transforming
relationship with the divine.

But your marriage proposal is nothing like
a new worldview, or a tradition, or a religion,
and I'm not really sure how we've managed
to reduce it to those things.

If your story doesn't stir me,
if your truth doesn't change me,
then the disease in my soul
is more severe than I thought.

Do whatever it takes.
Unafflict me.

The Road to Siloam
(John 9:1–7)

I heard them talking.

I heard what they were saying and I'm wondering if maybe it's true that I'm this way because God is punishing me. Either for something my parents did or something I did long ago, before I was born.

Or something I'm doing right now.

So maybe they're right.

But he told them no, that a bigger reason was at work, and I wondered if his hint was a riddle or a promise. Then he touched me. With mud on my eyes and strong words in my ears, "Go to the Pool of Siloam," he said. "And wash."

And so I left him. In the darkness I've always known, I left him. And now I'm on the road wondering why I did.

When I started walking toward the pool, I was thrilled, excited, hopeful. I really thought he might be able to do something for me no one else ever could, but the truth is, with more steps came more doubt. Maybe it was all just another joke that the seeing people were playing on me. All a game to mock the man born blind.

The people around me, the ones I've been asking for directions, they tell me I'm close.

So why am I still walking? I'm not sure. The trip has become something of an obligation. A way of going through the motions so that those who heard his words won't ask me, "So why didn't you go all the way? You never know. He might have actually opened your eyes."

I can hear the splashing water. The pool is just ahead.

Something will happen when I wash my eyes. Either my infant hope will die forever, or a new kind of life will be born.

They tell me I've arrived. The pool is at my feet.

I bend down.

I'm not proud of the trip, my doubts, my weak efforts to hold on to the faith I first had in his words. But now I'm here.

My fingers tremble as I reach forward and feel the cool water swirling, swirling right in front of me.

It's either simple water, or a mystery as deep as my past. All I need to do is wash. That's what he told me to do.

I don't know what will happen.

As I lean forward I feel a flicker of fear that I've made the journey for nothing.

And so now, my hope and doubt mix together into a fumbling prayer as I dip my hands into the water.

And lift them to my face.

you want to crucify
every part of me
that does not desire
to be close to you.

this is called love.

Hope-Giver,
I wonder what it would be like
to give you all of myself.

To dream of you,
hope in you,
depend on you,
live in you,
for you,
and with you,
without distraction.
To really give you what you ask of me—
my all, my everything.

I wonder what it would be like
to love you with all of my heart,
pursue you with all of my strength,
seek you with all of my will,
lean on you with all of my trust,
dive into you with all of my emotions,
my humanity,
my spirit's desire,
my soul's wide embrace.

I know it's what you ask,
but I tend to hold back parts of my heart.
It seems harmless when I do,
but my soul becomes poisoned without
your constant cleansing.

I wonder what it would be like
    to love you as you love me.
I'm willing,
but I'll need your help.

Today I offer you my heart,
my life,
my all.

i disappear into my hermit life
surrounded by untamed desire.
what a small and untidy room
this is.

O Great Revealer,
maybe I'll spend today dusting off my trophies
and moving my diplomas closer to
eye level.

I know, I know, one day
they'll be in a garbage dump
and I'll be in a grave,
but still, redecorating
might be a fun way to spend
my afternoon.

    I wonder how often these antics
    bring you to tears.

And I will give you treasures hidden in the darkness—
secret riches.
I will do this so you may know that I am the LORD,
the God of Israel, the one who calls you by name.
—Isaiah 45:3 (New Living Translation)

O Dawn of the Future,
your way of redeeming the night is to offer
secret riches,
hidden treasures
that can only be found in the dark.
Reveal them to me.

When you speak,
you untangle my thoughts
from the grip of the night.
Dawn unfurls,
and sunlight lands with a dancing splash,
like golden dew upon my face.

if the wise touch you with their minds,
and the clowns with their smiles;
then make me the biggest fool
in the carnival of your kingdom.

King of the Path,
Lamb of the Cross,
Sacrifice of Heaven,
Prince of Fools,
Wonder of the Stars,
Weaver of Eternity,
remind me how
wonderfully,
awkwardly,
frighteningly,
gloriously
I am made,
and how alive
and in love with you
I can actually be.

It is always springtime in the heart that loves God.
—John Vianney

God,
I revere you,
and I honor you above myself;
  above all else.

I give you the credit
  for the good parts of my life;
and I take the blame for the bad.

Glory.
Fame.
Praise to you.

You're patient in the ways
you deal with me.
You pursue justice
in the corners of the world I ignore.
And you show compassion, even to those who
  take advantage of you for doing it.

You are deep and mighty—the source of all strength.
You are glistening goodness—the source of all love.
You are lovely beyond all loveliness—the source of all
  beauty.
Wonder and truth, marvel and mercy
fall from your fingertips.

It sounds a bit clichéd, but
I adore you, O Lord,
you are precious to me.

I'm awestruck by this universe
that you spoke into being;
and humbled whenever I think of
your tender mercies toward our planet
and your intimate concern for me.

the crust around my heart
begs for the hammer.
be gracious to me;
swing harder this time.

Creator of Curiosity and Wonder,
you call for us to be celebrators of all that is good,
admirers of all that is just,
proclaimers of all that is true,
pursuers of all that is pure,
participants in the great mystery,
citizens of the great kingdom,
servants of the gracious, loving,
terrifying, Prince of Peace.

Being fully human looks different
than I expected.

your invisible love
shows me a different color
of truth—
and lights the dying
twilight of my heart.

To the one who is completely perfect and pure.

Two voices inside of me.
Two voices.

I will let them both speak to you—
  the one that wars against the world,
and the one that carefully stays in the crosswalk.

I will let both voices speak to you—
  the one that raises the gun,
and the one that offers a plateful of rice
to the AIDS-dying-orphan
in the garbage dump
that is his home.

I will let both voices speak—
the wrong one and the right,
the darkness and the light,
the Hitler and the Gandhi,
the rapist and the saint,
since all of them live inside my soul
and poke their heads out at different times.
I will let both voices speak,
so that I can see both faces of myself—
both faces of the world,
and let you guide me
toward the one and
  away from the other.

here is the mystery:
angels cry and demons laugh
and God sits on his throne.

To the source of all that matters.

"We need a place to worship," we say.

"You already have plenty," you respond.
 "Hospitals and nursing homes,
 street corners and homeless shelters,
 prisons and schools and slums."

Remind me that you never asked us
to build a building,
only to build a kingdom
by showing raw and real compassion
to a lost and lonely world—
 by feeding the hungry,
clothing the naked,
visiting the imprisoned,
comforting those who suffer,
 welcoming the weary,
and sharing the good news of your kingdom
with those willing to listen.

Let me change the place I worship
to the temple you've provided,
all around me in my everyday life.

the galaxy's heartbeat roared.
and the bloody story began.

conception.

Author of Life,
let more of your kingdom come to earth
reign in hearts, open eyes, quiet anger,
dispel worry, spread light,
  break the backbone of religion,
erase regret and comfort the shattered.

We need fewer family values
  (whatever those are),
and more Jesus-values.

More courageous humility,
mettlesome mercy,
bold compassion,
unsettling honesty,
  and unashamed, unrestrained marvel.

A place where wealth isn't hoarded;
where children are welcomed
  (and listened to),
where the humble inherit the earth,
the grieving discover a unique kind of happiness,
and reconciliation is more important
  than sacrifice.

A kingdom where the only things
we should mask from others

are our prayers, our fasting,
our tithes, our good deeds.

Where adultery can happen with a glance,
and murder can happen with a thought,
and only forgivers receive forgiveness.

Where we give to everyone whatever they ask,
power belongs to the meek,
the most persecuted are the most blessed,
sorrow is wedded to joy,
and light shines from people's lives
    and not just their glossy words.

Today I step unashamed
into the world of
cheek turners,
enemy lovers,
eye-plank removers,
door knockers,
truth seekers,
and narrow gate finders.

A place for the undead, unlost,
undeceived, undamned
    sinners like me.

some people hide themselves in religion.
you hide yourself in my heart
so that i can finally
stop hiding.

Source of Living Water
is it true that I want you?
Or is it maybe truer that
deep down
    in the secret place
I don't want you as much as
I want the rewards you offer?
Do I come to you for what you give,
or for who you are?

Are you just an ulterior motive
to get what I really want?
If that's the case,
don't give me what I want.
Give me yourself instead.

Some people honor you, serve you,
so that they can get a crown in heaven.
I would rather spend eternity
conversing with the king
than trying on crowns.

Let knowing you be the only reward
I ever seek.

i hover around your flame,
each day drawing closer into the sweet death
you call life.

Eternal God,
teach me about the endlessness of time:
the living without dying,
the breathing without fearing,
ways of your children.

Your wisdom stretches
beyond the farthest star
and wraps around the universe.
Your love calms the galaxies
and quiets my heart.

Bring me up to speed on infinity,
and then show me how you've
already packed it all into
this present moment.

my gypsy soul wanders into town
and makes its rounds again.

Holy One,
back when I walked away from you
I planned to return,
  really, I did.
It wasn't supposed to be a long-term thing,
just a little vacation.
You know.

But since then
things have become a little more complicated.
I guess I sort of settled in here.
It's not that bad of a place, actually,
in fact it's starting to feel just like home.

Vacations can do that,
change the way you look at things.

So I guess what I'm trying to say is,
I think I'll probably stay here for awhile.

Don't worry
it won't be for forever.

Wherever the Holy Spirit is present,
people of clay are changed into people of gold.
—from *Homilies on the Acts*
of the Apostles 4 by Chrysostom

To you.

I'm used to poking around
the rubble of my crumbled dreams,
but now I see that you're the one
smashing them to pieces.

You're the one holding the sledgehammer
in one hand
and an invitation to the palace,
in the other.

why do i think my life
should be filled
with cream and cookies
when yours was filled
with blood and tears?

To the one who prayed in the garden.

You offer a type of joy I didn't expect.
I expected happiness and ease;
you handed me
both anguish and ecstasy,
both peace and anger,
both thanksgiving and shrieking pain.

I'm finding that
the longer I follow you,
the more my heart is broken by
the things that break your heart,
and the more enraged I become
    at the things that enrage you.

Help me to become more like you
in the things I enjoy
    and the ones I despise;
and help me to show people
that following you is
much more than living the
smiley-faced caricature of Christianity
that seems so popular these days.

if i look at you and weep, i am saved.
if i look at you and yawn,
i have joined the legion of the damned.

and if i look at you and raise my fist,
i am on my way to the truth.

To the one who brings wholeness and purity.

When I'm wicked
and when I'm holy,
then I am most alive.
But when the fire becomes coal,
when my passion dulls
and my apathy hatches,
well, those are the times I enter into the slow death
of indifference.

I think you prefer the scalding hatred
of your enemies to the lukewarm
assent of those who claim to be your friends.

When I slip into apathy, my soul
awakens as a zombie.

Free me from the complacent
dailiness of living.
Set loose your disquieting fire,
pour on the gasoline.
Inflame me again.

teach me to listen to the stillness
but never to still the laughter.

Source of Peace and Meaning,
my life so often seems so cluttered and full,
so stressed out and full of worry,
and urgency,
and deadlines I just can't seem to meet.

There are so many expectations and obligations
tugging at me from so many different directions.
I get frantic.
I get anxious.
I tend to default back to busyness.
And the truth is,
sometimes I want to just hang it all up
and bail on my work and my family,
and maybe even my life.

Help me to take steps to simplify
and stop accumulating more stuff
that I don't need and don't even use.

Lord, please give me more simplicity,
more silence,
more trust,
more contentment.
Give me the courage to embrace quietness
and let peace sweep over me again.

Serenity is the gift you offer
to all who stand before you
with open hands.

sometimes i need answers from you
and sometimes i need mysteries.
why do you always seem to give me
the one i'm not asking for?

O God and Spirit of Eternity,
I came to you for comfort and guidance
and you told me tales
of tombs and blood.

I was hoping for a little encouragement here,
a little reassurance that I was being
good enough and trying hard enough;
but instead, you talked about
slaughtered lambs and unfaithful brides
and serpents and gardens of choices and tears.

One of us has things a little mixed up here.
That much is for sure.

every breath is a miracle—
but wonder this deep is easy to miss
when there are so many
sitcoms to watch.

God,
I'm ashamed to admit it, but here's my typical prayer:

"God, make my life safe, comfortable and easy. Lead me away from the trials that might purify my faith, the difficulties that might teach me perseverance, and the temptations that might reveal my true allegiances. Please don't discipline me (even though I know you say it would shape me into the kind of person you desire) because it might not be very pleasant and I want my life to be Happy and Fun All the Time. Be for me a Santa Claus or a Dr. Phil, not the battle-hardened warrior of the ages or the fiercely loving Father you are. Amen."

No more of those prayers, God.
I promise.
For your sake and mine.

i said,
"what type of wedding is this anyway?
prostitutes don't marry princes.
except in fairy tales or hallmark movies."

and you said,
"those are the only kind of weddings
allowed in the kingdom of heaven."

To the one who is worthy of praise.

In your kingdom
no one is more mature than a child,
or bolder than a lamb,
or more profound than a carpenter,
or freer than a slave.

In your kingdom,
fools tutor the wise,
the weak lead the strong,
death is swallowed by life,
and love tastes like pain.

If I could wrap my mind around you
then I know you would most certainly
be too small to wrap new life
around me.

Here in your kingdom,
I find a frail and innocent terror,
a stunning and time-washing grace.

Let glory fall on me
and crush me until
I learn to inhale
kingdom air.

cramped as i am in this
broken womb-world;
i once again begin
squeezing through the birth canal
toward the thing i fear most—
life.

Redeemer,
I look into the face of
the grinning skull that I will one day
be reduced to, and in my empty
eye sockets I see the
dim reflection of
today.

With every step I take,
remind me that death
is on my heels,
but that you are in my heart.

Bethlehem has opened Eden: Come, let us see! We have found joy hidden! Come, let us take possession of the paradise within the cave.

—from the anonymously written
Ikos of the Nativity of the Lord

Jesus,
I want to be close to you,
to stand naked before you,
stripped of my pretenses,
my ambition,
my illusions.

I want to close my eyes to myself
and open them to you,
to live with you unashamed,
  undistracted,
in perfect awareness and clothed with joy.

This would be heaven to me.

you rip out my cold heart
and offer a beating one in its place.

why do i fight such ruthless love?

God,
I know that envy is the secret cancer of the world,
but still,
I don't like it when you give me the diagnosis
in such a blunt and candid way.

"I'm going to have to remove that growth
or it'll continue to spread."

"But will it hurt? I mean if we decide
to go ahead with the surgery?"

"For this surgery, I can't use any anesthetic.
So yes. I'm afraid it will hurt very much."

"But what if I don't have the growth removed?
Will it hurt then?"

"Actually, after a while, it won't hurt at all anymore.
You won't even notice it. Not at all."

And so,
I stand staring at the operating room door
trying to decide what to do.

Aristotle was asked, "What things should an intelligent person acquire?"
He replied, "Those things which will swim with you when your ship sinks."

—from *Living a Good Life*, translated from the Greek by Thomas Cleary

To the one who reaches out to me.

I heard the words they said at her funeral
and I wondered why no one said those things
to her while she was still alive.

I'm thankful you didn't wait
until too late before telling me
how you feel.

you are the great puzzle-solver
who is constantly working
to piece me together.

Eternal One,
you shaped my soil-skin
    moist beneath your fingers.
Now I feel your breath pass across
my graveyard heart.

The early days of creation
were only a prelude to what
you do for formless, vagabond
souls like me,
when your Spirit comes
to hover,
    and create.

Why, then, be fainthearted in my hopes? Why believe like a mere creature of the day? I await the voice of the archangel, the last trumpet, the transformation of the heavens, the transfiguration of the earth, the liberation of the elements, the renovation of the universe.

—from *On His Brother Sr. Caesarius 21*
by Gregory of Nazianzus

To the great companion.

I tend to bury myself in the urgent,
the trivial,
the quickly fleeting nonsense
of my harried,
hurried life,
until there's no room for you.

I'm an expert at coming up with
elaborate ways to distract myself
from the things that matter most.

I'm running as fast as I can and
every hour is another frantic stride.
I used to think I was running toward you,
then for awhile I thought I was running away from you.
But in truth you've been running beside me
this whole time.

you left your fingerprints on the world.
i know; i've seen them. you can't hide from
me that easily.

To the refresher of my soul.

You fashioned an empty place
in my heart and said,
"This emptiness, this longing, this need,
is the greatest gift I could give you."
It is the only hole in the world
that was meant as a gift."

So I lay myself before you:
a damaged heart in need of repair,
an empty vessel needing to be filled,
an aching soul needing to be healed.

I cling to your promises of comfort,
and ask that you give me
guidance, strength, and peace
as I lean my life in the direction of
your will.

a smear of heartaches
rubs through my life.
my soul itches in all the places
that i can't seem to scratch by myself.

To the one who is just and merciful.

When you're inexplicable in my favor—
like when I'm healthy, or have straight teeth,
or don't get migraines, or cancer, or rabies
or dandruff,
I don't really tend to notice.

But when I'm on the other side of your
unfathomable incongruities,
I have the audacity to call life unfair.

How did I ever drift this far from thankfulness
into such blatant self-pity?

my choices drive the splinters in,
and the stark wound of grace
is the only thing that heals.

Master,
I've noticed that I have dark
undertows of regret and shame
running through my life.

Sure,
most of the time I'm able to keep them hidden
far beneath the surface
where my friends
aren't expert enough to swim.
But sometimes the currents rise
and unsettle
me.

Unless I get caught I rarely change direction.
Redirect me now,
    while the waves are still visible,
before I become afraid again.

> *The sun goes out*
> *whenever the cloud of not-praising comes.*
> —from *The Rumi Collection*

Bend down, O Lord, and hear my prayer;
*answer me, for I need your help.**

Dad, c'mere. Please. I need to tell you something.

Protect me, for I am devoted to you.
Save me, for I serve you and trust you.
You are my God.

I'm scared, Dad. I'm scared of the dark and of monsters and I've never really told anyone about it before. You're strong. You can protect me. I trust you.

Be merciful to me, O Lord,
for I am calling on you constantly.

Don't be mad. I need you and I don't know where else to turn.

O Lord, you are so good, so ready to forgive,
so full of unfailing love for all who ask for your help.

I love you, Dad. I'll do whatever you say. I promise. Whenever I'm with you, I feel safe. You make me happy.

I will call to you whenever I'm in trouble,
and you will answer me.

From now on, whenever I'm scared, I'm gonna talk to you. You're the best dad in the whole world.

Amen.

*These readings are from Psalm 86:1–7 (New Living Translation)

life is a breath
a mist, a tree losing leaves in the autumn.
you are the steady day
refusing to bow to the coming night.

Mighty One,
you came,
star to flesh,
flesh to light,
light to lamb,
lamb to corpse.

Here in your life,
I find the stir of a promise,
the cry of a child,
the flight into Egypt,
the mysterious boy,
the troublesome rabbi,
the body and the blood on my tongue,
on the cross,
in the grave,
and then—
a life-opening day,
a new kind of dawn,
a scarred and risen God,
a final conclusion that's
actually
only the beginning
of the real story that
you've been waiting all this time
to tell.

You moved through
grave and hell
to dawn and day
to become my Brother,
    to become my Lord,
the great and glorious
Galaxy King.

I bow before you
and close my eyes
and marvel at your tale.

we are sky children
lost in the valley,
looking for the trail
back up the hill.

To the one holding the key.

Somehow I've managed to convince myself
that all of these chains I drape over my soul
are really necklaces to happiness.

It's hard to have perspective
when the prison feels so much
like home.

Lord of the Brokenhearted,
how can i swallow your love
without tasting the rusty
flavor of a young carpenter's blood?

God of Fire and Grace,
you offer love
that knows no bounds,
forgiveness that pardons the lost.

Pour your presence into me,
fill me with passion,
then consume me with your Spirit's
hungry flame.

Take me wherever you want,
change me as you wish,
mold me into the shape
  of your dreams.

Break through the comforting
illusions of my life
and bring me something
terribly, wigglingly, writhingly real.

with a heart this full of lead, it's
no wonder i need you to
keep me from sinking.

Holy Spirit,
I wish I knew myself as you know me.
It would make my need for you clearer,
my awe of you sharper,
and my love for you greater.

Begin the process.

Start unpeeling the layers of illusion
that I've clothed myself with.

My self-deception is so comforting,
 and so destructive.
Freedom only comes as you reveal
more of my darkened heart to me
 and as I offer more of myself to you.

you offer me fire-laced freedom
and blood-bought pardon,
and i turn you into a
passing topic of conversation.

God,
I thought I should probably let you know that
a demon showed up at my doorstep yesterday.
He was returning my shadow-clothes.

Apparently I left them at his place
when I stopped by for a visit last week.

So, to make sure they hadn't shrunk,
I tried them on
and found that they fit just
as snugly as ever.

I'm telling you all this because I noticed the outfit
that you set out for me on my bed.
And I'm curious,
are you trying to get me to revamp my wardrobe?

Truth is,
I'm pretty comfortable with the clothes I already
have.

Just let me know what you're up to
so I can decide whether or not
to try on those glowing clothes
waiting for me in my room.

you make me more and more uncomfortable
until i'm finally ready
for your kind of comfort.

Mighty God,
the harder I try to hold you down,
the more you wrestle from my grip.

You're such an elusive lover.
You don't try to tame or be tamed,
control or be controlled—
it's as if you only want to set me free
so that I can choose on my own
to leave you or to love you.

What kind of love is that?
A love that actually trusts the beloved?

Hold me again.

I'll stop trying to tame you,
trying to control you,
and instead I'll let you teach me
the truth about the liberty of love.

If we say, "We aren't sinful,"
we are deceiving ourselves,
and the truth is not in us.
—1 John 1:8

O Great Forgiver,
O Great Forgetter,
I entered this world a virgin
in so many ways.

But my life has been a procession of one night stands
with Resentment
and Arrogance
and Impatience
and Unforgiveness.

I've had so many affairs
and lost my innocence
in so many areas.

It's funny, in a tragic sort of way,
how we lose so much in life
by clinging to it, and there are so
few ways to feel pure and untainted again.
In fact, you might have offered the only way
when you offered yourself.
In life.
In death.
For me.
To bring your cleansing,
renewing spirit
to my wayward heart.

You are a mad God
lavishing your crazy love
on someone as promiscuous as me.

I run to your arms again.

let this be the only legacy i leave:
the vapor of a life
that smells like you.

Holy One,
let truth go before me,
let wisdom walk beside me,
let compassion live within me,
    and let charity flow from my hands.

You chose poverty
    to bring me wealth.
You chose pain
    to bring me hope.
You chose distress
    to bring me joy.
You chose the cross
    to bring me a different kind of life.

Conquer me with your
sweet invasion.

Let all that is not born of God within you die.
—Francois de Fenelon (1651–1715),
priest and Christian mystic

Christ,
here is the pre-born, ingrown prayer of my life,
the one I am finally unlearning,
finally unpraying:

Midnight, O Midnight,
take me to the club
where music throbs to a primal beat.
Take me down the street.
And to your room.
And love me there,
in your silken bed
draped in satin dreams,
and filled with screaming ecstasy
forever.

So now,
here is my new prayer:
O Gracious One,
burn away the darkness
that remains in me from
all the times I've danced with,
and followed,
and slept with
the night.

Make us children of quietness, and heirs of peace. Enkindle in us the fire of thy love, strengthen our weakness by thy power, bind us closely to thee and to each other in one firm and indissoluble bond.

—from the Syrian Clementine Liturgy

Mighty Deliverer,
the kingdom life is
one of faith rather than sight,
simplicity rather than extravagance,
moderation rather than indulgence,
sacrifice rather than acquisition,
and a step in the direction of God
  rather than into the
soul-numbing security of my own agenda.

Make these truths personal.
Make them mine.

I find that when I bend my life toward the truth
I can feel the truth bending back,
supporting me, giving me the delicate strength
  and intimate balance I need,
and washing me from the inside out.

Only the hand that erases can write the true thing.
—Meister Eckhart (1260–1328), Christian mystic

The farmer sighed, "I don't understand why God doesn't hear my prayers. I've prayed and prayed for rain to fall on my crops. But none has come. Without rain my family will die."

And each day he would return to the fields and hold up seeds of grain in his outstretched hands and raise his prayer to the empty sky, but the rains didn't come.

His friend just shook his head. "There must be something in your life that hinders your prayers. Perhaps sin or doubt. I myself have prayed for no rain at all to fall. And see how God has answered my prayers?"

"What? When did you start praying your prayer?"

"Yesterday."

"But the drought has already run its course. Why pray now?"

"Rather than ask God to enter our plans, we should enter his," said his friend. "It's always better to find out what God's will is and then pray for that, than to trust in what you think is best. And it just goes to show that there's nothing in my life that's hindering my prayers."

"Then pray with me for rain so that my crops and my family will be saved."

"No," he said, turning his back. "I have some very important matters to attend to and don't have the time right now."

So, the farmer searched his soul to see if there was anything that would hinder his prayers. And he found both sin and doubt. *Maybe if I confess my sin, God will finally hear my prayer,* he thought.

And so, he confessed his sins and prayed again for rain. But it didn't come.

He gave God his doubts, but still no rain came.

Finally, he stopped offering his prayers and gave up believing in his God. And he cursed the heavens for not listening to his requests or his confession.

And that very moment, the clouds began to roll in and the rain began to fall on the hard and dusty ground.

The next day his friend returned smiling. "See? Once you got rid of the sin in your life, the rains came. Just like I told you they would."

And the farmer went away and wept.

His friend watched him leave and then looked up at the churning sky and said, "I believe it's time for me to pray for rain."

my heart is not as daring as your
desire, and so i shrink back again
into the quiet twilight
of hesitating faith,
where i slowly fade to black.

Promised Savior,
you love to whisper through the stillness,
but I've noticed that you're also pretty good
at shouting to me in the storm.

Following you isn't that strenuous,
as long as you don't ask me to step out of the boat.

But you do.

the only pathway
that is not a mirage
is faith.

Dearest Jesus,
all too often I give you a small part of my life
and then set about convincing myself that
what I've given you is enough.

I could use some more of your presence,
some more of your mystery,
rising out of the water around me,
glistening in the sun, splashing wildly
    through my life.

Sometimes I turn to food or sex or work
to
fill my soul.
Why do I expect the visible to heal the invisible?

A soul this damaged can only be bandaged
by your hand.

You are my hiding place;
you will protect me from trouble
and surround me with songs of deliverance.

Many are the woes of the wicked,
but the LORD's unfailing love
surrounds the man who trusts in him.
—Psalm 32:7, 10 (New International Version)

God of Unconquerable Love,
here is your promise:
you sing around me,
you surround me with love.

Today I'm going to remember that
and I'm going to take you at your word,
whatever else might surround me—
the small things like computer problems,
car trouble, bad weather, bad breath,
and endless Viagra spam,
and the big things
like depression,
persecution, grief, and guilt.

Whatever may try to overpower me,
I'm surrounded by something more powerful—
your unfailing love woven
into a glorious song of deliverance.

If you want to be loathsome to God, just run with the herd.
—Søren Kierkegaard (1813–1855), philosopher

Son of God,
and Son of Man,
temptation tickles me,
titillating
me,
exciting and thrilling me,
  especially when it's
played out in the
sexy side of the soul.

Part of me wants to say,

> "I may try a small tryst now and then.
> Nothing serious, mind you.
> Just a brief chance to sow my wild oats."

Or,

> "Oh really? I didn't know you were
> serious about that, God.
> No, really, you actually meant
> what you said about obedience?
> Well, next time I'll know better.
> Next time things will be different.
> Trust me."

These are the words I ask you to burn away
from my heart
in the refining fire of your love.

no matter how many times
i rinse out my mouth,
the aftertaste of the
forbidden fruit just won't
go away.

Heartbeat of the Universe,
hell is so lonely, not because you aren't there,
but because no one notices you
or wants to;
because making things better for themselves
is all that the residents of the inferno
care about, even though it's a task
that proves to be eternally futile.

For some people, hell starts here
in the middle of another busy
and important day.

I've seen its shadow mark the faces
of the living damned.

Heaven is when we finally see
how close you've been to us all along.

scarred by wonder and grace
you are the glorious twilight
of the day that is always dawn.

"This is the greatest treasure a wise man ever had," said the angel who spoke to me.

"What is it?" I asked.

And he drew a dagger from his belt. "It is the Dagger of Truth."

"Is Truth a dagger?" I gasped. I had thought truth was perhaps a blanket to cover your nakedness, or a meal to nourish your soul, or a harmony to calm the future. "Could Truth really be a dagger?"

He nodded and handed me the blade. "Its sheath is Wisdom," he said. "Wisdom will tell you when to wield Truth and when to keep her safely and quietly by your side."

I wondered at such a magnificent gift, but then I cut myself as I placed the Dagger of Truth into the Sheath of Wisdom.

"I've wounded myself with the Truth," I cried, as the blood spilled from my hand.

"Then you should be thankful," said the angel.

And before I could say another word, he was gone.

if i am already seated with you
in the heavenly realms,
why am i so worried about
phone calls,
traffic jams,
and how to deal with my
  bad hair days?

and i hear you say,
  "because you are also seated there
  in the earthly realms,
and that's just part of the deal."

Mighty and Gentle Creator,
if you know my every need and
keep track of every follicle of hair that falls,
does your love count the pebbles of sand
  and number the drops of summer rain?
Do you time each rainbow and track the path of
  every seed?
Do you orchestrate the interplay of autumn wind
  and every tumbling cloud?

When I start to wonder if the details of my life
really matter to you,
remind me of how you clothed
the flowers.

His compassion is never limited.
It is new every morning.
His faithfulness is great.

My soul can say, "The LORD *is my lot in life.*
That is why I find hope in him."

The LORD *is good to those who wait for him,*
to anyone who seeks help from him.

—Lamentations 3:22–25

Lord,
new mercies were born this morning.
I heard the eggs cracking when I woke up,
saw their tiny heads
poking through my regrets.

I think I'm going to pick one up
and carry it with me through today.

Who knows. By tonight it might be fully grown.

And be carrying me.

left to myself
i drift away from you
and toward
myself.

Mysterious and Triune God,
I create images of you in my mind,
but my vision of you is blurred
by my perception of myself.
I have a heart tainted with selfishness
so I see you through the lens
of what I want you to be
and not the lens of who you really are.

Unclutter my faith.

Give me a broader,
truer understanding of who you are,
even if it will be more frightening
and more comforting
than I can stand.

The abyss cannot understand the song of the stars.
—from *A Treasury of Kahlil Gibran*

O Majestic One,
I tend to ignore
the songs of the hills
and the praise of the peaks and the plains.

Sky and sun and desert sand,
    moon, eclipse, and raging sea,
join in the never-ending song.

The dancers sway to the silent beat
as melodies sweep the canyons and
harmonies top the hills.

The music throbs with joy and sorrow,
rising into a wondrous and daring
shout of your praise.

How can I so often miss hearing
the canticles of the gulls
and the worship of the ancient waves
when their concert
is always in session?

You've equipped eagles to soar in praise,
stars to wander the night,
worms to burrow their love,

I want to join the song.

Open my eyes to see the earth's uplifted hands
    and my ears to listen to it calling your name.
Help me to hear the psalms of the galaxies,
    and the poems of the whispering stars.
Help me to hear the worship all around me,
the prayers of the sunlight and the pine
and the glistening morning dew
    right outside my window in my own front yard.

if God didn't exist
i'd be an atheist.

Jesus,
when I have you, I lack nothing,
and all I need accomplish is to rejoice.

Give me neither poverty nor riches,
but give me only my daily bread.
Otherwise, I may have too much and disown you
and say, "Who is the LORD?"
Or I may become poor and steal,
and so dishonor the name of my God.
—A prayer of Agur son of Jakeh
(Proverbs 30:8–9, New International Version)

"This is how you should pray . . . Give us today our daily bread."
—Jesus of Nazareth (see Matthew 6:9–11)

Father of All Creation,
Lover of All the Earth,
I wonder how many financial advisors pray Agur's prayer
for their clients every day.
It just seems so un-American to pray like this.

After all, nearly every investment strategy,
money management system,
budgeting plan,
is designed to help us short-circuit
this prayer of Agur son of Jakeh.

We prefer the Prayer of Jabez—
"enlarge my land,"
to this Prayer of Agur—
"limit your blessings because I am weak."

Nobody wants to live day-by-day,
Mouth-to-mouth.
Except maybe those in the kingdom:
a kingdom where we only ask for daily bread,

and not contingency plans
or savings accounts,
or safe investments,
or 401k plans.
    Let bread for today be enough.

i say, "i am a slave to no man," and so
i reveal my chains;
i say, "i am a slave to you,"
and i hear the cell door swing open.

Spirit of Freedom,
the winds have picked up lately
so I've been using my sails more.
But now I'm starting to realize
that the current is tugging me back toward
the shore I left when I first climbed aboard
your boat.

Don't let me return there.

I hear the call of the far horizon,
and so I adjust my sails to welcome
a new kind of wind. Fill them,
as I turn to face the open sea.

i get to know you through
studying religion
about as much
as i get to know my bride
by doing an autopsy
on her corpse.

Lamb of God,
I smell blood
on the skin of the world.

Blood.
Dripping from your wrists,
landing on my cheek.
Here before me I see
the fresh sacrifice
of my slaughtered God
splattered with hot,
crimson
blood.

Blood.
On my conscience.
On my hands.

I keep trying to wash it off
but it refuses to go away.

I was the one who willingly drove the nails
into your outstretched hands.

Forgive me.

if john the baptizer
wasn't fit to untie your sandals
i can't even imagine
what i'm unfit to do.

Jesus,
they tell me
it's not enough to "talk the talk,"
that I need to "walk the walk."

But the truth is, I'm having a rough time with that
because I keep stumbling all the time.

Is it really hypocrisy to just
talk the talk, or could it be a small step
toward finally walking the walk?
I knew the truth and yet
falter at times. This doesn't seem like
hypocrisy to me. It seems more like
weakness. More like human nature.

Even if I haven't been
able to live out all of my convictions,
please know that when I offer myself to you
it's my way of reaching
out so that you can
help me take another step.

With each new day
let striding within your will
become more and more
my natural gait.

thanks for trying life.
please enjoy before the expiration date.

Lord,
disappointment wraps around my feet,
I can feel myself getting pulled down
by my past once again.

I remember the soft waves,
the brilliant sun,
the clear sky,
but right now the day around me
is draped in fog and sorrow.

Lift me up,
set me free,
unwrap my sadness,
pull the veil away.

Let me see the world again
shining in your blazing love.
Part the clouds,
wash me of my past.

All it takes is a touch of your mercy,
your stillness,
your welcoming grace,
and I will no longer be sinking
so far into myself.

i look across my life
and see so many storms.
i look across your love
and see only horizons.

To the patient one.

My fears don't really make sense.
Sometimes I'm afraid of failing,
other times of succeeding.

I'm afraid of trusting you
but also of living without you;
afraid of being alone,
and also of being too dependent.

I enjoy feeling like I'm in control of my life,
but when I realize I've never been in control at all,
fear creeps in again.

Yet even with all of my
doubts and misgivings, you still care about me.
I matter to you,
and you speak to me
within my failures and my fears,
whispering your gracious love into the
confused universe
of my life.

You're the only thing I need to fear,
and the only one who can
drive all my fears away.

whenever i hear your story,
darkness is impaled by the truth;
and the more the shadows bleed,
the quicker dawn arrives.

To my Father.

I'm on my way home again.
I know the way, but it's been a long time.
I'm different now—
not much older, but much more wrinkled.
Funny how things change us,
funny how we change things.

You loved me enough to let me leave.
It didn't seem like love back then—
honestly, it seemed like indifference.
But time has taught me more
about what real love looks like.

Now,
I see my old house up ahead
waiting tentatively beside the road.

And then you appear,
without folded arms or a furrowed brow,
just outstretched arms and tender tears.

You run to greet me,
looking past my past.

Even though I ran away willingly
and came back grudgingly,
you loved me enough to wait for me,
and now I feel the greatest love of all
as you welcome me back home.

> *I have come that they may have life, and have it to the full.*
>
> —Jesus of Nazareth, explaining why he came to earth (John 10:10, New International Version)

To the one who came to free prisoners.

You dance on the breeze in the evening light,
you leap on the curl
    of a wave, crashing white.
You twirl on a star in the darkest night,
calling, "Live the journey! Live!"

You seek out the path of the summer rain,
you gleam in the sunlight
    and bound through the grain.
You shout through the storm and I hear the refrain,
"Live the journey! Live!"

You ride on the clouds as they streak through the sky,
you soar with the eagle,
    and gleam in her eye.
You call from the peak and the mountains reply,
"Live the journey! Live!"

You brave all the rapids and paddle upstream,
embracing the world's
    most impossible dream.
You whisper and shout, and sometimes you scream,
"Live the journey! Live!"

You stand with your face to the salt and the spray,
you run in the race
    in the heat of the day;
you invite us to die and be born a new way;
to live the journey.
To live.

i need you to help me
position the knife
as i commit ego suicide.
again.

To the one who provides for my needs and inspires my desires.

They say, "Discover your own truth."
You say, "I am the truth."

They say, "Find your way in the world."
You say, "I am the way."

They say, "Follow your dreams."
You say, "Follow me."

They say, "Live your own life."
You say, "I am the life."

They say, "Find yourself."
You say, "Come unto me."

It is astonishing how much
depends on which voice
I choose to listen to.

Lord give me ears
to hear the shrieks of the world,
and the courage
to press my hand against its wounds.

O Light of the World,
a single word from your lips
can scatter the deepest darkness.

So say the word,
break through the stillness,
change my heart that I might seek you,
change my mind that I might know you,
change my eyes that I might find you,
change my ears that I might hear you,
change my life
that I might
actually,
finally,
truly,
fully,
live.

i run away from you
so that i won't feel so lonely.
that's how lost i am.

To the one who knows the path.

I hear you speaking to me:

"Listen."
I have.

"No, I said listen."
How?

"Stop trying so hard."
You mean give up?

"Yes."
Oh.
OK.
Then what?

"Close your eyes and listen."
To what?

"Me."
Um.
OK.
Then what?

"If you were really listening you would already know."

the love of heaven
walked down my street
but i didn't recognize her
because i was expecting her
to look just like me.

Author of Grace,
I used to know what peace felt like.
And purity.
And innocence.
But now, once again, filth and regret have crept in
to the place where my faith used to sleep,
and excuses and lies have nestled in
where honesty used to live.
It's become easier for me to sleep with my illusions
than with you,
but in moments like these,
I realize how much I miss the intimacy of your
embrace.

O Lover of My Soul,
hold me in your arms again.
I'm back from the streets and the darkened alleys
and the cheap hotels.
I long for the love that only you can give.
I'm back, and I need you again.
I divorced you when I left for the city,
now I'm ready to divorce myself.

who are the ones
who are truly insane?
the madmen and poets and
prophets who scream in the night,
or the rest of us
who
sleep through all of our days?

To the living God.

My life is consumed with balancing the scales and making sure I don't owe you anything and that I've paid up and I'm not in debt to anyone so that I can Feel Good About Myself,
just like the preachers of self-esteem tell me to feel.

But sometimes it's tough because I do things I shouldn't feel good about, and then I have to be nice for awhile to balance the scales, or I might remember a time someone hurt me
and then I can say,
"See! Now we're Even!"

Anything so that I don't have to admit I was wrong.
Anything so that I can keep up this façade and continue to claim that I am
Only Human,
and have a right to
Make My Share Of Mistakes.
Because I couldn't stand to admit that I really am terribly less than I should be and much more evil than I have ever dared
to admit.

I vacuum in the praise and I shovel out the blame.
and that's how I keep the balance in my life.

i'm trying to catch up with myself.
but the faster i run, the
more of myself i leave behind.

To the one who is three; to the three who are one.

I know of only one way
to make sense of my senseless life:
    disappear into the love
flowing from your words.

Your story tells me all that needs to be said,
fills all that needs to be filled,
restores all that has fallen apart,
    and heals all that has been infected
with selfishness and greed.

The world is confusing
and even though my questions
pester me, I see that everything
will make final, perfect sense,
but only when I look
into the laughing, illuminating
light of your eyes.

Mystery.

my deepest scars
aren't the ones left by my friends
or my enemies,
or even by you.

my deepest scars are the ones
i've carved into myself
when i thought i was wounding someone else.

To you.

The truth is,
I don't really care anymore.
I don't care if I'm being petty or selfish
or trivial or apathetic
or complacent
or whiny.

I like holding grudges
and sometimes I enjoy getting on people's nerves,
and I'm not really all that
excited about going on
a missions trip or
giving to my church's
new development campaign.

I'm tired of being good.
I don't want to go to church,
or forgive people,
or trust in Jesus,
or pray.

I used to get excited about worshiping you,
but now, it's all dull and lifeless.
Life as a believer seems boring.
I don't want to confess my sins,
or sing your praises,
or have anything to do
with this whole Christianity-deal
anymore.

So what happens now?

at the end of myself
lies the beginning of the journey.

O Potter,
left to myself, I begin to dry in the
awkward shape of my past.

Give me a supple soul,
one that's soft and responsive
to your shaping hands.

And if you need to,
shatter me to pieces
and start over
with fresh clay.

i keep a list of other people's wrongs,
taking note, keeping track.
    "ah, ha!"
now i'm armed for battle.
wrong me and i'll never forget.
never!

    so i will always be enslaved.

To the river flowing with joy.

Search me, O God, and know my heart.
Search me from the inside out,
look deep into the real me,
inspect me.
Even though it makes me uneasy to be examined
so closely, I need you to do it,
to perform the great unveiling.

Expose the excuses I've fallen in love with
    and slice them from my life.
Find the darkened corners of my heart
    and bring them light.
Uncover the empty places of my soul
    and fill them with yourself.

Hammer my excuses to pieces.
Don't give up until I'm helplessly,
desperately clinging to you
again.

i sink in the quicksand of myself
so frequently
that i've started to feel at home
here in the swamp.

To the one who brings troubling peace.

Sometimes I get sick of life.
I become discontent,
dissatisfied,
frustrated,
worn out,
exhausted,
and just plain fed-up with it all.

So often I feel overwhelmed
and weary of fighting my way
through another day.

I get restless,
my passion dies,
my motivation disappears,
and I find myself criticizing people
rather than encouraging them,
and becoming jaded
rather than more and more thankful.

Maybe I've lost my faith.
Maybe I never even had any.

Shift my eyes from noticing the cracks in the path
to seeing the stars in the sky,
from focusing on the heartaches
to celebrating the blessings.

death has always been a fine hunter,
but on skull hill she found
her prey hunting her.

Master Storyteller,
in your kingdom,
a kiss conquers a curse,
a peasant girl becomes a princess,
and all the orphans in the village
are invited to move into the palace.

On your lips,
the old tales take on new truths,
the story of my life takes on new meaning,
and the words "happily ever after"
invite me into an infinitely freeing
"once upon a time."

Churches offer me weekly documentaries on religion,
but all the while I'm living in a deep fantasy,
pursued by an ancient dragon.
Where did we go wrong and turn
the grand tale into a lesson?

Here's my life story.
Retell it
with the transforming power of your words.

gluttony is the blinding vice of our times.
we eat ourselves sick
while children starve to death next door,
and then we get offended
when people call
us fat.

King of the Lost,
I breathe in the fragrance of your Spirit
and it sweeps through my soul,
touching all the hidden currents,
filling all the deep crevices.

Cleanse me,
purify me with the truth that frees,
the truth that breathes,
the truth that impregnates
infertile lives with infant life.

You don't hold my past before me to accuse me;
you hold your story before me to pardon me.

You know everything,
you see the real me,
and you accept me as I am.

You love me with an extravagance I'll never
understand,
majesty circles out from your heart
and dives deeply into the soul of my surrender.

I lay down my arms.

gallop into the throne room
stop all this peering through the lattice
and quivering with uncertainty
the king will see you now.
  but only if you are willing
  to see him.

A prayer to the God I honor.

You said to pray for my enemies
and to bless those who curse me,
so right now I'd like to ask a blessing
on that guy who did some cursing at me
just the other day in his pickup truck
out on the highway.
And I'd like to pray for the people at work who don't
  like me,
  and the ones I don't like,
for the Republicans (or Democrats)
who drive me crazy with their idiotic policies.

I pray for those who would benefit from my failure:
  my competitors, other job applicants,
  the other people vying for the scholarship,
  the terrorists who want to kill me.
I pray for them all.
Bless them with more prosperity.
Give them more peace, less suffering,
more honor and success.

You said to bless those who curse you,
    the angry atheists
    Al Qaeda,
    the Taliban,
and the people all over the world
who belong to religions
that justify hatred and murder
    in the name of their gods.
Bless them with a truer sense of who you are,
and a greater desire to follow you.

Here they are, prayers so big
they have frightened me before,
intimidated me with their enormity.

If it's true that I can approach your throne with
    confidence
here I stand,
trusting that your power
is greater than my reluctancy to pray
and truly believe.

you barred the pathway back to the fatal fruit,
why do i try so hard to get back inside
that garden of serpents and thorns?

God,
I'm so full of pain I feel numb.
Life has swarmed over me again.
Suffering has touched me
in the deepest recesses of my heart.

I see my dreams collapse
and my hope drying out.

Maybe if I trusted you more,
I wouldn't feel so empty,
or worry so much,
or feel so crushed.

You're the one who suffered for me.
You're the one who died
on my behalf.
And in the Garden of Gethsemani
you're the one who felt
the most profound anguish ever.

You stepped into the pain of this world
so that I could step into the peace of the next.

You understand.
You can help.

If I have to suffer, let it be with my eyes on you.
If I have to be humiliated,
  let it be to make you famous.
If my heart is destined to ache,
  let that loneliness bind me closer
  to the center of your heart.

"The idea that God is everywhere, all the time,
is either the most comforting or the most unsettling
doctrine of all."

OK. So let me guess:
the only difference is whether or not he's on your side.

"No. The only difference is whether or not you're on his."

Lion of God,
Lamb of Glory,
this world is in need of saving,
and that's not going to come
by stopping global climate change.

We need saving from selfishness,
and spiritual blindness,
and road rage,
and the diversions that swallow our time,
and the tendency to hold grudges,
  and to wallow in guilt,
  and to look down on others.

We need saving from the hellbound road,
the angry, impatient, workaholic,
abortion-as-the-easy-way-out road.

We need saving from the hatred road,
the indifference road,
the addiction road,
the road that tolerates immorality and vice,
but does not tolerate disagreement.

And you showed us a new road.
You became the road,
when you became the way.

Heal us one at a time
so we can heal our world.

the trees on the edge of the forest
lean their branches toward the light.
and the only time i grow strong
is when i do the same.

O King of the kingdom that never ends,
you are concerned about me
and that makes me feel accepted.

I celebrate you.

I celebrate your favor toward me,
your precious tenderness,
your mercy,
your forgiveness,
your justice.

I celebrate your
gracious love,
your glorious name,
your unmerited acceptance.

I celebrate your power,
your world-crafting wonder,
and your soul-inspiring mystery.

I celebrate your
insights into what is best for me,
your wisdom, which is greater than I can grasp,
and your incomprehensible plans.

I celebrate your changelessness,
because it means that the love you had,
you have,
the forgiveness you offered,
you offer,
and the joy you gave,
you give.

I celebrate you
and am humbled and amazed that
you, the great and glorious
God of all that there is,
actually celebrate
  me.

i'm on a constant hunt for loopholes.
i want to thread them onto an elegant
necklace that i can wear
for eternity.
  knock them from my hand.

To the one who shapes stars and comforts
  broken hearts.

Sometimes I'm so discouraged
I don't feel like praying at all.

Whatever prayer is, sometimes it seems to help
and sometimes it doesn't.

Soften the soil of my heart.
Water the roots that are still there somewhere,
deep beneath the surface.
On my own, I become more and more parched;
with you, someday,
my petals might actually
  begin to unfold.

when i look at the lives of great sinners,
i see how much they need God.

when i study the lives of great saints,
i see how much they trust God.

and my greatest fear is that i'll
drift comfortably
through life without becoming either.

Friend,
break open my tamper-resistant life.
Give me more courage and more opportunities
to share your message with other people.
I'm quick to excuse my lack of courage
by pointing to my heritage,
    or my personality,
    or my lack of knowledge,
when, really, the problem is my self-concern.
I'm so obsessed with acceptance by others
rather than obedience to you.

I don't want to live a life on display any longer.
Help me to stop making good impressions
and to start making accurate ones.

Melt my clever rebellion.

Help me to make you famous in all the right ways,
and help me disappear from history
in the process.

People who cover over their sins will not prosper.
But if they confess and forsake them, they will receive mercy.
—Proverbs 28:13 (New Living Translation)

To the one who hears both my prayers and my complaints.

Sometimes I just want to scream at you,
"How could you let this happen?
Why? Why are you treating me like this?"

I want to tell you how much I love you
and how much I hate you;
how much I need you,
and how often I disregard you;
how much I want to run away from you,
and how much I never want to leave your side.

I feel this strange kind of fear—
a fear that is both humbling and comforting,
both terrifying and nurturing.

I don't just want to pray;
I want to step into that place
where I cannot help
but pray.

the final pregnancy is
slyer than the first.

those birth pains
led to life;
but these lead
to glory.

To the one who is worthy of honor and praise.

Thank you for imagination,
and laughter,
and taste buds.

Thank you for children
to remind me of hope,
for the elderly to remind me of respect,
for mountains to teach me to marvel,
and for starlight and rain to wake me up.

Thank you for the needs of others,
to keep me from obsessing about my own.

Thank you for the terror that leads to trust,
the anguish that leads to peace,
the shame that leads to forgiveness,
and the illumination that leads
to you.

Thank you for a universe
where mercy conquers pain,
and justice rules at the end of the day.

Thank you for giving me new perspectives
and for opening before me new horizons.

I love you,
and I lift all that is within me
to thank you for your grace.

Index

Steven James is a critically acclaimed author and award-winning storyteller. He has written many collections of short fiction, scripts, and inspirational books that explore the paradox of good and evil. He lives at the base of the Blue Ridge Mountains with his wife and three daughters.